John Coleman

FREEMASONRY FROM A TO Z

OMNIA VERITAS.

John Coleman

John Coleman is a British author and former member of the Secret Intelligence Service. Coleman has produced various analyses of the Club of Rome, the Giorgio Cini Foundation, Forbes Global 2000, the Interreligious Peace Colloquium, the Tavistock Institute, the Black Nobility and other organisations with New World Order themes.

Freemasonry from A to Z

© Omnia Veritas Ltd – 2023

ⓄMNIA VERITAS.

www.omnia-veritas.com

Freemasonry is often described as a "secret society," but Freemasons themselves believe it is more correct to say that it is an esoteric society, in that certain aspects are private. The most common phrasing being that Freemasonry has, in the 21st century, become less a secret society and more of a "society with secrets." The private aspects of modern Freemasonry are the modes of recognition amongst members and particular elements within the ritual. For instance Masons might ask newcomers they meet "are you on the square?"

In an open society such as the United States, one is left to wonder why the need for secrecy? The task of describing Freemasonry is a daunting one. Saying that it is the largest fraternal organization in the world with over 3 million members in the United States and seven hundred thousand in Great Britain and a million more around the Earth, and that it has been the study of fifty thousand books and pamphlets is only the beginning.

Since it was revealed in 1717, Freemasonry has engendered more hatred and enmity than any other secular organization in the world. It has been constantly subjected to unremitting attack by the Catholic Church, its membership forbidden to men of the Mormon Church, the Salvation Army and the Methodist Church. It is outlawed in a number of countries.

Anti Masonic allegations always run into difficulties because Masonry refuses to respond to attacks. What is surprising is the very large number of world leaders, past and present who were and are members of Freemasonry: King George VI of England, Frederick the Great of Prussia and King Haakon VII of Norway. U.S. history is replete with leaders who were Masons such as George Washington, Andrew Jackson, James Polk, Theodore Roosevelt, Franklin D. Roosevelt, Harry Truman, Gerald Ford and Ronald Reagan.

WWII was fought by British Masonic leaders such as Winston Churchill and the American President Franklin D. Roosevelt, and American army leaders like Generals Omar Bradley, Mark Clark and George Marshall. It is virtually impossible to know where to begin or to end in recounting Masonic influence on every aspect of life for the past 290 years. This work is an attempt to put together that which will make it relatively easy to explain "What is Masonry."

CHAPTER 1

WHAT IS FREEMASONRY?

The study of Freemasonry is an inexhaustible one, and many books and learned papers have been written and presented in regard to the subject; therefore it is not my intention to go into the highways and byways of Masonry and get lost down side lanes and tracks in a maze of rituals and symbols, which have mostly been covered in any case by those who are for, and those who are opposed to Masonry.

The purpose of my message is to give you a broader insight into what Masonry is, what it stands for, what its aims and objectives are, and how far it has progressed toward its stated goals. For this reason, I shall be dealing first with speculative Masonry, that part of Masonry dealing with spiritual matters of life and death and the human spirit, and who controls with a brief explanation of craft Masonry.

For details of rituals and ceremonies, I have drawn on such Masonry reference works as Royal Masonic Encyclopedia, or as it is sometimes called Cyclopedia. For an account of where the greatest pro-Masonry advocates have spelled out their ideas, including Albert Pike and Dr. Mackey, as well as in books and journals written by staunch enemies of Masonry; men like Abbe Barruel, Professor John Robinson, Eckert, Copin-Albinecelli and Arthur Preuss, to name but a few learned men who are named by Masons as "our implacable enemies." (Strange that the Jesuits should use the exact same phrase.)

The origins of Freemasonry have been argued over for more than 150 years. According to Pike:

> ... The origins of Freemasonry are known only to Freemasons.

Pike indulges in wishful thinking here. His claim is intended to deceive the unwary and it is rather typical of the deception which Masonry practices, something like falling into the hands of a magician and not knowing how he performs his illusions.

The origin of Freemasonry is, however, very well known; it is no secret, no mystery. But it is also certainly true that the majority of Masons, who never rise above the 4th Degree, do not know the origin of the society whose dictates they so slavishly follow.

Dr. Mackey, recognized as a Mason's Mason, the spokesman for Masonry, admits this. Its chief defender, J. F. Gould, confirms that much disagreement exists among Masons themselves as to its origin. This is to be found in his work, The History of Freemasonry. Contemporary research shows its origin is found in Babylonian and Egyptian mysticism, coupled with Black Magic.

It is a religious cult, dedicated to the worship of Lucifer. It is anti-Christian and revolutionary in character, even as its master, Lucifer is the symbol of rebellion against God, a rebellion, which has continued for thousands of years.

The world owes its knowledge of Freemasonry to Professor John Robinson, one of its most illustrious members who defected from its ranks, and thus a man whom the Masons cannot call a liar or confound. Professor Robinson taught at the Royal Society of Edinburgh, Scotland. His subject: Human Philosophy. Robinson was deeply involved in secret societies, the principal one being the Bavarian Illuminati sect of Adam Weishaupt.

Robinson was a 33rd Degree Mason; that is to say, he had reached the top of the tree in the Order of the Scottish Rite Freemasons.

In 1796, Robinson published a paper, which set out the aims of the Illuminati, proving that the Illuminati closely paralleled Masonry. In fact, Masonry was the vehicle used to spread revolutionary Illuminati doctrines, starting in France.

Robinson proved beyond dispute that the aim of the Illuminati and Masonry is to destroy all religions and governments and to eliminate Christianity from the face of the Earth and replace it with Luciferian worship.

The New World Order promised by Freemasonry is a despotic, Luciferian One-World Order inside a One-World Government. A complete set of blueprints for the coming revolution fell into the hands of the Bavarian government, who were deeply alarmed, so much so that it sent copies to every government and head of state in Europe, only to have its message of warning completely ignored.

The Weishaupt documents gave full details of the coming French Revolution. Masonic Order devotee, the Earl of Shelburne, taught and trained both Danton and Marat (the radical leaders of the French Revolution) and directed every phase of the "French" Revolution from England.

CHAPTER 2

ORIGINS OF MASONRY

Babylonian Gnosticism is the mother of Freemasonry, which is why the letter "G" figures in the center of Masonry's five-pointed star.

In spite of furious denials by the defenders of Masonry, no lesser an authority on Masonry, from its highest Order, Eliphas Levy said the "G" signifies Gnosticism. In his work, Dogme et Rituel de la Haute Magie, volume II, page 97, Levy says:

The "G," which Freemasons place in the middle of the flamboyant star, signifies Gnosticism and Generation, the most sacred words of the ancient Kabala.

The Kabala is ancient Jewish mysticism, according to the Encyclopedia of Religions, and Brother Edersham, an authority on the Kabala. Now, I do not want to go into the byways, as I stated before, but it is necessary to very briefly establish what the Kabala is.

To this end, I quote the authority, Brother Edersham:

It is undeniable, that already at the time of Jesus Christ, there was in existence an assemblage of doctrines and speculations that were carefully concealed from the multitude. They were not even revealed to the ordinary scholars (just as in the case of higher doctrines and ordinary Masons) for fear of leading them towards heretical ideas.

This kind bore the name Kabbala as the term indicates (i.e. to receive and to transmit) it represented the spiritual transitions transmitted from the earliest ages, although mingled in the course of time, with impure or foreign elements.

This is the very same Tradition of the Elders, which Jesus Christ utterly condemned in very strong language as recorded in the Four Gospels, the record of His spoken words during His earthly ministry.

It becomes clear from the foregoing, that Masonry evolved from a religion utterly opposed to the ministry of Christ, thus it follows that in spite of its vehement denials, that Masonry is anti- Christian in teaching and in spirit. Others implacably opposed to Masonry, as mentioned earlier, go even further. An absolute supreme authority on Masonry, Copin-Albancelli, said:

Freemasonry is the counter-church, the counter-Catholicism, the church of heresy.

He quotes several notable Masonic sources to back up his contention such as Copin-Albancellis, Bulletin of the Grand Orient of France, September 1885, as declaring:

We Masons must pursue the Catholic Churches utter demolition.

I was privileged to be able to research documents on

Masonry in the British Museum in London to see whether this statement and others which follow herein, have ever been withdrawn or retracted. But over a period of five years of intensive search, I was unable to discover any Masonic publication containing a retraction of its destructive intentions toward the Catholic Church.

Yet another example cited by Copin-Albancelli is the memorandum of the Supreme Council of the Grand Orient (European Masonry), which states:

> The struggle being waged between Catholicism and Masonry is a war to the death without truce, without quarter.

This statement has never been retracted.

Copin-Albencelli goes on to give further examples, quoting as his source the address given at a summer solstice banquet in 1902 by Brother Delpek who said, inter-alia:

> The triumphs of the Galilean has lasted twenty centuries. May the Catholic Church die in its turn... The Roman Catholic Church, founded on the Galilean myth (a reference to Jesus Christ) have begun to decay rapidly, since the founding of the Masonic Association? From the political standpoint Masons have varied frequently. But at all times, Freemasonry has been firm in this principle: War on all superstitions, war on all fanaticisms!

The foregoing information, beyond dispute genuine, makes Freemasons and Freemasonry anti-Christ and anti-

Christian, dismissing His teachings in the most disdainful manner possible as a Galilean myth and superstition. Their pent-up hatred and venom is directed mainly toward the Catholic Church, yet there are some who say that Catholics aren't Christians. Believe me; were this to be true, Freemasonry would not be spending 99% of its time and energy in trying to destroy the Catholic Church? Why would Masonry waste such precious time and so much energy? Let us be logical about such matters.

The above should leave no doubt about where the hierarchy of Masonry stands. It also clearly establishes that Masonry is politically involved despite its frequent protestations to the contrary. If we summarize the conclusions to be drawn from the above statements, then we can only arrive at one judgment: Masonry is essentially an untruthful, deceitful and deceiving secret society, in which the bulk of its members are borne along on a tide of banquets, social get-togethers, good works, goodwill and philanthropic fellowship. The sinister character of Masonry is completely hidden from the mass of its members, that is to say, those who do not progress beyond the Blue or Fourth Degree.

According to the learned Dom Benoit, a superior scholar of Masonry, whom even the Masons acknowledge had great knowledge of their secret speculative oracles, Masonry is devil worship. Describing initiation ceremonies of the 25th Degree, (Knight of the Brazen Serpent) initiates swear to work for the return of man to Eden. The Master mentions the serpent as a friend of man while our God—to whom Masons refer as Adonai or Adonay—is listed as the enemy of man.

Benoit says that in the 20th Degree, the inference of

Luciferian worship is even more positively stated, because the presiding judge says to the initiate:

In the sacred name of Lucifer, cast out obscurantism.

Obscurantism is one of the few key words that will make any Mason above the Fourth Degree foam at the mouth, when mentioned in his presence by someone who is not a Mason and therefore, not supposed to know the word and its significance.

As I have said before, many Masons who are professing Christians "once you know these mysteries, can there be any room for doubt, that Masonry is the adoration of Lucifer and the denigration of Christ."

Benoit has a further, more damning indictment against Masonry, which he stated in the following manner:

Who is credulous to believe that after so many serious and constant affirmations, that Masons respect all religions, that the preoccupation with religion and the hatred of the Catholic Church exists only in certain Masonic Degrees, in which they say of Christ, that He is a fallen angel. I have seen the emblems of one of the Grand Lodges, which is a chalice bearing an image of the host pierced by a dagger, another, the world with the cross upside down, and still another, the Heart of Jesus with the motto "Cor Ex Secranrum" on it.

In a discourse of the Luciferian Palladium Rites of Albert Pike for the Elect of the Reformed, Benoit states that the initiates are instructed to "punish the traitor Jesus Christ, to kill Adonai by stabbing the host after being assured that it is a consecrated host, while reciting horrible blasphemies."

Pike was born in 1809 and died in 1891. His book, Morals and Dogma, confirms the worship of Satan and his belief in a New World Order. He had disdain for any political system that was a republican limited government with democratic principles. Political power, wealth, health and long life were to be gained by the worship of Lucifer, according to Pike.

The book talks very much in favor of homosexuality, with the cover showing a double-headed eagle. It is clear that the central theme of the book is to destroy morality and family. The book condemns Biblical morality and the family, the cornerstone of civilization.

Now I know, there are those, even high Masons, who are going to say " ... we have been Masons all of our lives and have never witnessed such a ceremony." Of course not! That is standard procedure for Masonry; only the elect are initiated into these rites. If you have not progressed beyond the 25th Degree, you will not be aware of these vile anti-Christ rituals! And let me warn you, that any attempt to elicit confirmation of Benoit's claim from the Mason hierarchy will mean that your days as a Mason are numbered. You will thereafter be a marked man, not to be trusted.

To quote Brother Stroether, yet another recognized authority, one who has never been challenged by Masonry simply because he was one of their own from their inner councils, a man who used words that have come back to haunt Masons:

Masonry exists in France, Spain, Portugal and South America as an anti-religious organization, which in the last years has developed into a kind of antithetic sect, which makes no secret of its hatred for revealed religions.

Brother Stroether was a member of the elect, a high degree Mason from Louisville, Kentucky in the U.S. I asked a number of high degree Masons to comment on the words of Stroether. Without exception, they either profess ignorance of who Brother Stroether is, or else they deny, that he said anything of the kind. A particularly outraged Mason, a State Trooper Colonel in North Carolina told me, "This kind of comment is the product of a diseased anti-Mason mind."

But when I confronted him with the words of his own Masons, he warned me that I would be well advised to leave Masonry alone. The words that had upset him were those uttered by the infamous Paul Lafargue (1842–1911) during the 1866 International Congress of Grand Orient Masons at Brussels, Belgium:

War on God! Hatred to God! In the progress it is necessary to crush Heaven, as if it was a piece of paper.

At the same conference, a notable Mason by the name of Lanesman repeated the words used in 1880, viz:

We must crush the infamous one, but that infamous one is not clericalism, that infamous one is God.

CHAPTER 3

HISTORICAL ENEMIES OF MASONRY

I have diligently researched the documents from which these excerpts were taken to confirm their accuracy. Moreover, with equal carefulness, I researched Masonic files in the British Museum in London looking for retraction and or disavowal of these profanities by higher Masons; but nowhere did my search yield any evidence whatsoever, that these words are not the creed of Masonry in general, nor that they have been withdrawn.

A well-respected Masonic leader, who confirmed everything stated thus far, especially the anti-Christ nature of Masonry, was its high priest, Albert Pike, co-founder of the New Palladium Reformed Rites and Supreme Pontiff of U.S. Masonry. Albert Pike and Edgar Allen Poe had much in common. Both were born in Boston, in 1809. Both were writers and poets and both were opium addicts, as well as being 33rd degree Masons and Luciferians.

In the Catholic Encyclopedia, we read that Albert Pike and another important high-ranking Mason, Adriano Lemmi, conspired together to harm the Christian religion in Italy. Pike wrote Lemmi as follows:

> It is necessary to ruin in a short time, the clerical influences in Italy, the laws against the religious

congregations are to be observed there. And (what of) the schools? Catholic instruction is always given in them. Make people protest by means of the lodges.

In other words, use Masonic lodges to instigate "protests" against the Catholic schools.

Professor John Robinson spent many years carefully researching the exposure of Masonry presented by Abbe Barreul.

Robinson states:

> Barreul confirms all that I have said of the Enlightened, whom he very aptly calls Philosohist and the abuses of Freemasonry in France.

> He shows unquestionably, that a formal and systematic conspiracy against religion was formed and zealously pursued by Voltaire, d'Alembert and Diderot, assisted by Frederick II, King of Prussia, and I see, that their principles and their manner of procedure have been the same as those of the German atheists and anarchist... But their darling project was to destroy Christianity and all Religion, and to bring about a total change of government.

Robinson was discussing the undoubtedly vital role played by Masonry in the French Revolution, as was disclosed by Abbe Barreul in the most precise and indisputable manner. If this is not enough evidence for doubters, then let them turn to the most important "passwords" in Masonry. One of them is based on Cain, whom Christ condemned as a slayer of prophets in St. Matthew 23. The password, Tubal

Cain, is a very explicit reference to Cain. The other "secret word" is INRI, "Igne Natura Renovatur Integra"—"All Nature is Renewed by Fire" which is used to describe Jesus of Nazareth. The initiate is supposed to "discover" what this means, which gives an insight into how infantile are the rituals engaged in by Masons.

Then the Master of the Lodge declares:

> My dear brethren, the word is found, and all present applaud the discovery, that He whose death was consummation of the Christian religion was no more than a common Jew crucified for His crimes. It is on the Gospel and the Son of Man that the Candidate is to avenge the brethren the Pontiffs of Jehovah.

This quote is taken from the work of Abbe Barreul dealing with the 18th Rosicrucian Degree. The Rosicrucians were Masons, who founded English Masonry. It is fair to say, however, that the vast majority of English Masons never progress beyond the Fourth Degree, and heatedly deny that the foregoing exists. In fact several English Masons said that they were staunch Christians, and would never take part in blaspheming Christ or His church! Masonry for the majority of its membership is nothing but a repetition of the First and Fourth Degrees. It is no wonder, that so many give up at this point and make no attempt to go further. According to the very pro-Masonry Dr. Mackey, an authority on Masonry:

> ... These are the explanations and the High Degree is the commentary.

There are those who say that if Masonry is so evil, then

how is it, that so many Anglicans and even a few of the Popes were Masons? I agree that perhaps thousands of Anglican Church leaders are Masons, but these men are not Christians; they are underground agents of Lucifer, sleepers in place in the Church whose function is to destroy it! Can we say that "a few Popes were Masons," when it cannot be proved even though there is a strong suspicion that at least three Popes might have been Masons? Suspicion is not proof. A false rumor, begun among Masons in Germany, that Pope Pious XI was a Mason soon shifted to Philadelphia. Eckert, one of the supreme anti-Mason authorities tells us that this was done to avoid a follow-up investigation of the claim, which would have been easier to promote in Europe than in the U.S. Nevertheless, the claim was thoroughly investigated by John Gilmary Shes, the man who wrote extensively about the life of Pope Pius XI.

Shea's research proved that Pius XI had never been a member of the Philadelphia Lodge. In fact no such Lodge ever existed in Philadelphia! Preuss, another famous seeker after Masonic truths, confirms the plot, as nothing but an attempt to smear Pope Pius XI and the Catholic Church in general.

In reply to the often-asked question: "What is Masonry?" I can do no better than quote the great scholar and Mason historian Abbe Barreul… It is a most vile malignant evil, a view confirmed by Supreme Pontiff Albert Pike, who said:

> Blue Degrees are no more than the outer door of the Temple portal. Part of the symbols received are the same, but he is intentionally deceived with false interpretations.

It is not intended, that he should understand them, but rather that he imagined himself to understand them. Their true interpretation is reserved for the Initiated Ones, the Princes of Masonry.

These words appear in documents about Pike held by the British Museum's inner sanctum, if they have not been removed in the meantime, as are so many documents when they once become a source of reference for investigators of Masonry. There must be something "malignantly evil" in a society that sets out to deliberately deceive its own members. Copin-Albancelli, the note Mason historian, states that Masonry is an occult-directed force being used as a battering ram against the Christian religion.

CHAPTER 4

ENCYCLICAL MIRARI VOS, POPE GREGORY XVI

In this encyclical, Pope Gregory issued an order that Masonry is:

> ... Everything which has been most sacrilegious, blasphemous and shameful in heresies and in the most criminal of sects has been joined together in the secret society as in a universal sewer.

No wonder I get disturbed when people tell me, "Catholics aren't Christians." Show me where it is written that any Protestant leader has ever come out as strongly against Masonry as the Catholic Church has. I have not found one to this very day.

Perhaps this helps to explain the fact, that Vladimir Lenin was a Mason. Preuss says of Brother Lenin that he belonged to a secret lodge in Switzerland, under his real name, Ulianov Zederbaum, from which secure and protected base he strove mightily to bring about the overthrow of Christian Russia, an endeavor, I might add, in which he was most successful, thanks to massive help from Round Table Masons, Lord Palmerston, Lord Milner and a host of English 33rd Degree Masons. And yet, the Swiss government called this archfiend an "intellectual." This really makes sense when we know that for centuries, the home of Freemasonry has always been Switzerland. The "fraternity" showed in the case of Lenin that Masons stick together especially in endeavors, where the object is the destruction of the Christian religion, as in the case of Christian Russia.

The fact that English Masons made billions of dollars out of the rape of Russia was of course an added bonus. The real satisfaction was in the overthrow of Russia and the wholesale slaughter of Christians (certified as 60 million), which became a model to be followed in the Spanish Civil War (July 1936-June 1939). I refer to June of 1939, because that was the month that Franco marched in triumph through the streets of Madrid having smashed for God and country, the Luciferian forces of Communist-Masonry in his country.

A renowned authority I have not yet mentioned was Margiotta, who was initiated into the Palladium Rites and became a "Prince of Masonry." Margiotta said that Pike ordered the god of Masonry to be called Lucifer, much against the wishes of his brother-Mason, Adriano Lemmi, who desired that the Mason god be named Satan.

Albert Mackey says that Masonry is here to establish a New Universal Religion. The publication, A Cause, states that Masons must disregard all laws and authority in every country, exactly in keeping with the rebellious revolutionary nature of Lucifer, who rebelled against the laws and authority of God. Thus it can be held that by its own confession, Masonry is a revolutionary force, existing for the purpose of overthrowing the present order on Earth, just as its master Lucifer tried to overthrow the existing order of the Universe! Masonry is paramilitary order, as it's trapping and symbols, which are of a military nature, fully confirm.

Both Eckert and Benoit insist and provide remarkable proof beyond all doubt that the real authority in Masonry, the Supreme Command, is entirely occult in character, thereby explaining why the hidden Supreme Command shelters behind a mass of symbols and ceremonies, not to be uncovered until the highest degree of the Order is reached. Every effort is made to keep the identity (even to a change of names) of these secret leaders hidden from the ordinary membership, in a manner similar to that used by the Bolsheviks in Russia. (Is this where the Bolsheviks got their name-changing from?)

The 19th Degree of Scottish Rite Freemasonry declares:

> War on the Cross of Jesus Christ. Adopt the cult of Lucifer of fire and of flesh.

These vile words are a part of the proofs offered in Benoit's, *La Franc Maconnerie*, the most remarkable expose of Masonry available to those who seek knowledge about the true purpose of Masonry.

Three words cause 33rd Degree Masons to go into a towering rage:

> Catholicism, Obscurantism and Clericalism.

The second word is solely a Mason word, which they like to use to describe the teachings of Christ.

It clearly must have a double meaning to inspire the rage it does when used by non-Masons, because non-Masons are supposed to be ignorant of such words, and Masons hate to be unmasked. Masonry is a false brotherhood, since it deliberately excludes the poor and those who have no prospect of ever attaining political power and deliberately deceives its lower-order members.

CHAPTER 5

ECKERT POSES A PERTINENT QUESTION

Eckert poses this pertinent question:

Why does the Order exclude the poor, who have neither political nor economic value? It is a well-known fact, nor denied by Masonry itself, that they seek to enroll only those, who have made a success of business or political careers. The fact is money is the motivating force, when it comes to welcoming newcomers into the brotherhood.

Such blatant hypocrisy should sound a warning to any who may have been invited to attend one of the Masonic Temples in their area for a social get-together. This is the usual manner by which those whom the Order feels can be of financial benefit to it, do their recruiting. The Mason asks "Are you on the Square," meaning "Are you a Mason?" The questioner is fully aware through a secret handshake that the person he has approached is not a Mason, but someone he thinks would be likely candidate for membership in his lodge!

To deal with degrees and rituals would take a book of their own as there are hundreds of rites, many of them bordering on infantile.

There are many good works devoted solely to such rituals, which make for tedious reading. According to the Masonic bible, Encyclopedia of Freemasonry, and a newer book called The Meaning of Masonry, by W. L. Wilmhurst, the main rites are as follows:

- ❖ Ancient and Accepted Scottish Rite
- ❖ Rite of Herod
- ❖ Ancient Reformed Scottish Rite
- ❖ Grand Orient Rite (of which the French Rite is a part)
- ❖ Philosophic Scottish Rite (used extensively in Switzerland)
- ❖ Electric Rite (used a great deal in Germany)
- ❖ Rite of Mizraim (Ancient Egyptian Rite)
- ❖ Joanite Rite

It is interesting to note that the headquarters of Universal Masonry is in Geneva, Switzerland, under the title of International Masonic Association. Switzerland, as is well recorded in history, has always been a haven for revolutionaries.

A second "branch headquarters" is in Lausanne and it is a particularly secret one. Ascona is the home of Gnostic Satanist- Masonry-Communism. Remember, Masons are revolutionaries, taught to be rebellious against all existing governments, and Swiss Masons are no exception to this Mason injunction.

Benoit says of Mason rituals:

> ... They are long and tedious and exceedingly childish.

In order that their childish absurdities are not found out by "outsiders," before a Lodge meeting begins, it is "covered," a term used by Masons to ensure that no outsiders or interlopers are present to observe and report on the proceedings.

Eckert and Copin describe the goings on in various ways and use the term "unbelievable buffoonery" to describe it. The purpose of all this tomfoolery, says Copin, which involves secret passwords unknown to outsiders, and Hiram, (Hiram Abiff, King of Tyre) allegedly the builder of Solomon's Temple, who was slain, is to pull the wool over the eyes of secular authority, and make it believe that Masonry is a benevolent society devoted to banquets, collecting money for the poor, and generally doing good for the community! Copin says that in the Middle Chamber ritual, which a Master never enters, the members are required to march and counter-march "like school children."

Eckert goes on to say:

> ... We see in the ritual a theatrical presentation too serious to be a joke, too farcical to be serious.

Nevertheless, serious it is. The purpose is to weed out all those members, who quickly show they have no desire to progress beyond this point, from those who follow the ritual in a slavish manner. Hiram, of course, is the centerpiece. To them, the ladder up, which they must climb, is not leading to further folly, but to a higher and more trusted position in Masonry. It is interesting to note some of the titles to which the eager ones can perhaps one day aspire:

- ❖ 5th Degree - The Perfect Master
- ❖ 11th Degree - The Sublime Elect of the Twelve of Prince Ameth
- ❖ 16th Degree - The Prince of Jerusalem
- ❖ 19th Degree - The Grand Pontiff
- ❖ 28th Degree - The Knight of the Sun or Prince Adept
- ❖ 31st Degree - The Grand Inspector Inquisitor Commander
- ❖ 32nd Degree - The Sublime Prince of the Royal Secret
- ❖ 33rd Degree - The Supreme Pontiff Universal Masonry

The Rite of Herod particularly interests me. Why should anyone want to adore a murderer like King Herod, who killed thousands of newborn babies when the Magi brought him their alarming news of the birth of Christ? The only reason I can come up with is because Herod tried to murder the infant Jesus and the Masons are an anti-Christ Order.

But it is to the Princes of Masonry, those who have reached the 33rd degree, that the real face of Masonry becomes known. Adriano Lemmi, just such a Prince, revealed this in his explosion of hatred against family and church in his letter to Margiotta:

> Yes, yes, the standard of the King of Inferno is marching forward … and must combat today, more energetically and more openly than ever before all the artifices of clerical reaction.

Those, who slavishly perform Masonry's childish games and follow all ceremonial orders to the letter without missing anything, become known as "Brilliant Masons," which is two steps above the so-called "Knife and Fork Masons," who live only for the numerous feast and banquets Masons enjoy, while the non-qualifiers for a higher degree are called "Rusty Masons." Benoit says, the latter are also known as "Parrot Masons," because they know the lessons, but not the meaning thereof. There is absolutely no equality in the Lodges, which gives the lie to Mason protestations that all are equal, and that "liberty, equality and fraternity" is the cornerstone upon which Masonry is built.

Pike writes that the worship of Lucifer is known only to those, who have reached the final Degree. Lord Christopher Soames, the betrayer of Zimbabwe is such a person, as is Lord Carrington, the former Secretary General of NATO. (In the Congress of the United States we have many who are of the same mind as Lords Soames and Carrington. One who quickly comes to mind is Senator Trent Lott, a 33rd Degree Mason.) Copin, Benoit and Eckert all remind us, that the password Inri, which I have previously explained is a word hostile toward Christ. I wonder how Senator Lott and others like him who profess Christianity can square this with conscience.

What is Luciferian worship? We need to be clear on this point in order to understand Pike's Palladium Rites, and what it is the Princes of Masonry actually follow, while at the same time professing to be Christians, as in the case of many in the Anglican Church hierarchy, the aristocracies of Europe, not to mention the Eastern Liberal Establishment of the U.S. and many members of Congress! As explained by Albert Pike, Luciferian worship is a creed, which teaches that Lucifer was the brightest of God's three right-hand angels, a super-being endowed with super intelligence and capabilities. So great was his power that he was able to challenge God and take over the running of the Universe.

There followed a mighty battle with St. Michael, God's warrior angel (claimed by Masons as brother to Lucifer), defeating Lucifer and casting him out of God's presence.

Jesus Christ makes reference to this in the Gospels. Lucifer was banished to Hell, which is described as an actual place in the Universe. Lucifer took with him a large number of the leading angels in the hierarchy of Heaven, who were willing to defect with him. The Luciferian Creed holds that God gave these angels another chance to repent, because He considered that they had been deceived by the Master Deceiver, Lucifer.

For this purpose God created our planet and those angels who were deceived and not openly rebellious, were given bodies in God's own image and permitted to inhabit the Earth. These beings were filled with the breath of God and His spirit and light, and were sanctified by God. They were indistinguishable from ordinary people except that they had all knowledge of their previous life in Heaven blocked out. But they received inspirations from his word to sustain them on their plane and retained a free will. Their minds were used to decide from where the inspirations emanated and translate them into bodily acts, which are always either positive or negative—no middle ground. These acts are recorded in a book known as the Book of Life mentioned in Revelations.

By their actions in the physical realm, these beings of heavenly origin decide their own future, i.e. they could accept Lucifer's plan, or God's plan for rule of the Universe. One might say that it almost resembles what the Christian Bible teaches, but not quite.

Suddenly Satan appears, brought in by Lucifer, as the Prince of The World (Please note, the use of the word "Prince" is also used by Masons) at the moment of the creation of the world. Satan's task was to get the first parents to defect from God and join Lucifer, thereby spoiling his plan.

God, says Pike, walked in the Garden of Eden with his first son, but failed to instruct him in the pleasures of sex, because He is a jealous and selfish God. As taught in the lower Order of the Palladium Rites, God did this because such pleasure belonged to Him and was not to be shared until they had proved their obedience, integrity and absolute honesty. Only then would it be given to them as a reward.

Then, says Pike, Satan took a hand in matters and by the command of Lucifer inducted Eve into the pleasures of sex, which God had reserved for procreation, and which God had merely postponed telling the first parents about, until they were ready for it. Satan told Eve that she would be equal in power, as would Adam, to God, and would never have to go through death. Satan introduced Eve to what we are pleased to call "carnal knowledge," a term which is completely misleading.

Thus was the Luciferian ideal of free love and free sex introduced, as opposed to God's plan of sex inside the boundaries of marriage of one man to one woman for the purpose of begetting children, based upon a spiritual wish to bring about the Kingdom of God on Earth.

Pike's explanation of the Black Mass shows just how Eve was corrupted, and instead of sex being a personal and private physical and spiritual act of love, it was a public display of open sex with all-comers—which is the essence of witchcraft today. It is fair to say that given the conditions which prevail upon Earth today in the sexual realm, Satan is winning the battle, albeit temporarily until he was soundly defeated by Jesus Christ. Hence the unremitting hatred of Christ by the Masons!

CHAPTER 6

THE USE OF THE CHRISTIAN BIBLE IN MASONIC TEMPLES

P reuss and the Catholic Encyclopedia confirm the use of the Bible and the Cross in Masonic Temples. Many lower-Order Masons have challenged the statement made from time to time, namely, that Masonry is Luciferian worship. They say: "As we display the Bible and Cross, how can this be?" It is part of Masonry's deception plan. The Bible is only there to be held up to ridicule in the higher order, as is the Cross, which is actually trampled underfoot, while the most vile profanities are uttered against it.

Eckert confirms that the Cross and Bible are displayed to bring them down to the level of other religious "books" of little importance. In the 30th Degree of the Scottish Rite, the initiate is made to trample on the cross, while the Knight of Kadosh tells him: "Trample upon this image of superstition! Crush it!" If the initiate does not do it, he is applauded, but the secrets of the 30th Degree are not imparted to him. If he does trample on the Cross, he is received into the Knights of Kadosh, and instructed to execute his vengeance on three images representing the Pope, superstition and the King.

This graphic description is given by the renowned authority Benoit in his monumental work, *La Franc-*

Maçonnerie. Thus do Masons hope to advance the cause of Lucifer that he should rule the Universe. Some Masons have gone as far as having themselves emasculated, believing that unrestrained sex, as permitted by the Luciferian Creed, could very well interfere with their work in bringing about the Kingdom of Lucifer on Earth. Janos Kader, the former Hungarian leader, had himself castrated for this reason. The Catholic Church does not go to this extreme, but demands celibacy in priests and nuns so that sexual pressures cannot play any part in their service to mankind and to Christ. Pike, although a Supreme Pontiff, had his orders relayed to him through a set of "Instructions" in the year 1889, by what Margiotta says is a "Supreme Council Body of 23 Councils of World-Wide Masonry."

According to some translations of the text, which is in the British Museum in London, the Orders read:

> To you Sovereign Inspectors General, we say this, that you may repeat to the Brethren of the 32nd, 31st and 30th Degrees.

> … The Masonic religion should by all of us Initiates of high Degrees, be maintained in the purity of the Luciferian Doctrine. If Lucifer were not God, would Adonai whose deeds prove his cruelty and hatred of man, barbarism and repulsion for science would Adonai and priests calumniate him. Yes, Lucifer is God, and unfortunately Adonai is also God. For the eternal law is that there is no light without shade… Thus the doctrine on Satanism is a heresy, and the pure and true philosophic religion is the belief in Lucifer, the equal of Adonai, but Lucifer, God of Light and God of Good, is struggling for humanity against Adonai, the

God of Darkness and Evil.

This is the true religion of Masonry.

The aims and objectives of the Mason religion as outlined above are bringing about revolutions intended to overthrow the Kingdom of God on Earth. The overthrow of Christian Russia was a great triumph for the anti-Christ forces, their defeat by General Franco in Spain was a catastrophic blow in which Masonry was also pummeled, for which Franco will never be forgiven. If you think this is a tenuous connection, then think again; the Masonic plan for separation of church and state in the U.S. is tearing America apart, as is abortion, forced abandonment of school prayers, and Christians not being allowed to celebrate the holy days of Easter, Pentecost and Christmas correctly as national holidays. (Not in the manner of the Pagans with Easter eggs and Santa Clause etc!)

These are a few examples of what this doctrine has acknowledged. Mason pressure is a powerful pressure! Lest we forget, or indeed, lest some of us were never aware of it, Masons in France called for renewing ties with the Bolshevik government following a world-wide breaking of diplomatic relations in protest over the violence and bloodshed of the Bolshevik Revolution. Mason President Woodrow Wilson was the first to recognize the Bolshevik Government, in spite of strenuous protests by the Congress. The power of Masonry is awesome!

Eckert:

Masons engineered the First World War; they admit owing the most fierce insurgents and apostles of assassinations in the world.

The assassination of Archduke Ferdinand of Austria at Sarajevo, generally regarded by historians as the spark that set Europe ablaze in WWI, was a Masonic affair. There are many authorities besides Eckert who agree with the contention. From the explanation of the ritual as well as from secular history and confessions by members of the Order, one may rightly conclude that Freemasonry is a conspiracy against the altar, the government and property rights, with the objective of establishing all over the face of the Earth, a social theocratic reign, whose religious-political government would have its See in Jerusalem. The indispensable condition to this realization is the destruction of the three obstacles which are opposed to it, the Christian Church, government and private property.

The middle objection has largely fallen away. There is hardly a single government anywhere, where Masonry, if not welcome, is as least tolerated without let or hindrance. I often wonder, what it is about governments which allow this cancer in their midst to defeat all efforts to curb its activities. Governments cannot be blind to history, which is replete with examples of Masonic treachery. Why then is this devilish secret-society- Luciferian-religion allowed to exist in the very midst of this Christian nation? Why is any secret society permitted? I wish that someone better equipped than I, would explain this sorely perplexing question.

Perhaps it is due to the fact that governments in every Western country are fully controlled by a parasitic secret government, such as the one we have fastened around our necks, the Committee of 300, through its Council on Foreign Relations, which is absolutely Luciferian in every facet of its activities. In addition to this, we have many powerful religions which are not Christian, and indeed, one major religion is downright anti- Christian and it plays a leading role in all anti-Christian activities.

Masons regard the destruction of Christ as an essential goal of their religious purposes, which are of course fully interfaced with their political aspirations. America will yet pay a price for "freedom of religion" and the price will very likely be the total destruction of this great American Republic as we know it in its present form. If you open the doors to thieves, you must expect your house to be robbed!

The Masonic lie of "equality in all religions" has been exposed many times as quackery, specious mendacity, but it is worth repeating: In Masonry, there is no freedom of religion. None other than Luciferian worship is tolerated, and all others are undermined. Christianity, in particular, may fully expect an attack of utmost ferocity to be launched against it, when the Masons have gained power over all secular governments of this world as is their often-stated goal.

Naturally, Masonry does not broadcast its intentions from the rooftops of every city; indeed, as I said earlier, the majority of its membership is completely in the dark over these truths.

Again to quote the Supreme Pontiff, Albert Pike:

> Masonry, like all religions, all mysteries, hermeticism and alchemies, hides secrets from everyone except the Initiated, Sages or Elects, and employs false explanations and interpretations of its symbols to

deceive those who deserve to be deceived and to hide from the truth, which is called light and to separate them from it.

This very frank statement, which a number of Masons dispute as genuine, was verified by Preuss, one of the best authorities on Masonry, and is contained in the Pike papers in the British Museum in London. There is absolutely no doubt about the authenticity of this quotation.

CHAPTER 7

BRITISH ORIGIN OF NOTABLE DECEIVERS

The British have provided this world with many notable Great Deceivers. One such a notable who comes to mind was Benjamin Disraeli, one of its greatest Prime Ministers, although until the time he was picked up almost penniless by the Rothschilds, he hadn't amounted to much. But this is a story I have told in my book "The Rothschild Dynasty," one which has been revealed to only a very few. Disraeli is noted as an authority on Freemasonry, and long after the French Revolution was over made the following statement:

> It was neither parliaments nor populations, nor was the course of events that overthrew the throne of Louis Philippe… The throne was surprised by the Secret Societies, ever prepared to ravage Europe.

Now, I know this has often been quoted in the past, but I felt it worthwhile to include it in this book, simply because it is of no less significance today than it was when Disraeli uttered these words in 1852.

Make no mistake about it; the forces that ravaged France and Russia stand ready to ravage the United States. Will you not pay heed and see how South Africa was betrayed and sold out to the New World Order? If you will not pay heed then you deserve the fate that will likely overwhelm us all unless we can get the American people to wake up! I say this, because a study of American secret history lays bare the murderous, baleful influence of Freemasonry in the affairs of this nation. Both Presidents Lincoln and Garfield were assassinated by Freemasons. The assassinations were plotted and planned by Freemasons and it hasn't stopped there. President Reagan narrowly escaped death at the hands of John Hinckley.

There is absolute concrete evidence linking the Scottish Rite Freemasonry to the assassination plot. The psychiatrist, whom Hinckley first consulted, was a Freemason. Hinckley was programmed to commit the assassination, which failed. In short, Hinckley was as much brainwashed as was Sirhan-Sirhan. As reported in earlier publications of mine, the Hinckley psychiatrist, who later gave evidence at his trial, received a substantial "grant" from the Scottish Rite of Freemasonry. Need anything further be said?

For those who still think of Freemasonry as a philanthropic Order, dedicated to doing good, allow me to suggest that you read what Copin-Albancelli, a harsh critic, and Louis Blanc, one of Masonry's darlings, had to say about the Order. In a moment of frankness, Blanc bared the deceit of Masonry for all to see:

> Since three degrees of ordinary Masonry comprised a great number of men opposed, because of the status and principle for social overthrow, the innovators multiplied the degrees as steps to climb the mystic scale, they instituted the high degrees as a dark sanctuary, whose portals are not opened to initiates until after a long series of tests (which) are designed to

prove the progress of his revolutionary education, the constancy of his faith and the temple of his heart.

Blanc provided this undeniable fact; that Freemasonry is one of the strongest, revolutionary forces in the world, and has been so since its inception. Once again, we have to thank a Freemason spokesman for helping us to uncover the proofs needed to support the foregoing statement.

I have noticed how it is, that every time the Masons have a big banquet, one of them gets in his cups, and out comes the truth. Look at the statement made by the Freemason Jacques Delpech at a very big and important banquet held in 1902:

> The triumph of the Galilean has lasted 20 centuries, and he is dying in his turn. The mysterious voice, which once on the mountain of Epirus announced the death of Pan, today announces the death of the deceiver God, who promised an era of justice and peace to those who should believe in him. The illusion has lasted very long; the lying God in his turn disappears; he goes to rejoin the other divinities of India, Greece and Egypt, also Rome, where so many deluded creatures threw themselves at the foot of their alters. Freemasons, we are pleased to state, that we are not concerned with this ruin of false prophets.

> The Roman Church, founded on the Galilean myth, began to decline rapidly on the day, when the Masonic association was constituted... From this political point of view, Freemasons have often varied, but in all times, Freemasons have stood firm on this principle, war on all superstitions, war on all fanaticisms.

The original of this statement can be seen in the British Museum in London. I quoted an extract of this statement earlier in this book, but on reflection felt it advisable to include the full statement, because I consider it to be the most revealing words ever to be uttered by a high-ranking Freemason.

Perhaps less well known is the role played by Freemasonry in the War Between the States, also known as the American Civil War. An authority on the subject is the author Blanchard, who in his work, Scottish Rite Masonry, volume II, page 484, states with this regard to this tragic conflict:

> This is the most infamous Masonic war act, next to burning their records of 59 years before the war to hide treason. But slavery then ruled the country and the 33rd Degree Charleston ruled the lodge. And the Southern lodge rooms worked up the most unjustifiable and infamous war on record. The Southern people were dragooned into it by leaders, secretly sworn to obey Masonic orders and Masonic leaders, or have their throats cut!

What then, has Freemasonry achieved thus far? First and foremost, its war on Christ and the Church has been stepped up through a massive revival of witchcraft and the astounding spread of Gnosticism during the past decade (see my work, Satanism).

The struggle with the Catholic Church has also been intensified. By 1985, there were more Jesuits inside the higher councils of the Vatican, than at any time in the history of Catholicism. Its para-military Order, the Society of Jesus, has been able to fan out across the world and wreak havoc among nations, notably in Zimbabwe, Nicaragua, the Philippines and South Africa, and also to a very marked extent, inside the United States of America, where it has established a veritable fortress command center from where it has penetrated every branch of government. It has engendered a spirit of lawlessness sweeping the world in many forms, notably in the form of "rock" music and its twin, the drug culture, and in the sharp rise in international terrorism. It is a good thing to recall, that Christ said Lucifer stands for lawlessness and rebellion, of which he is the father. Reviewing the progress of Freemasonry, we look back to its first great triumph, the bloody French Revolution. Again, be reminded of the words of Christ; Satan is a murderer filled with bloodlust, and has ever been so.

Freemasonry played the leading role in planning and executing the French Revolution. For those of you who perhaps have not read it, I recommend the book, *The French Revolution*, by Nesta H. Webster. It is one of the best documented books proving beyond any shadow of a doubt, that the French Revolution was a Freemasonry undertaking, backed to the hilt by the Rothschilds, who expressed their longstanding, boiling hatred of Christ in this manner.

The same holds true of the terrifying Bolshevik Revolution of 1917. In both cases, we see the spirit of Freemasonry as the guiding hand, especially British Freemasonry. Prior to that we saw the Anglo-Boer War, a cruel and relentless attempt to wipe out a small pastoral nation of God-fearing Christians, the first act of genocide, carried out solely to take control of the mineral riches that lay beneath the soil of South Africa. Yes, it was the first recorded genocide against a nation. Leading Masons such as Lord Palmer and Alfred Milner carried it out against what they regarded as a "cheap" inferior nation (the words of Cecil Rhodes), the White Christian Boer Nation.

In that war we saw the first use of concentration camps and an all-out war against the civil population (as opposed to the military) resulting in the deaths of 27,000 women and children. The cruel Crimean War was another milestone in the progress of Universal Freemasonry.

The Abyssinian War, yet another genocidal war, came about simply as a means of ripping Italy apart and weakening the Catholic Church. It was nothing but Freemasonry intrigue from start to finish. General Rodolfo Grazziani was a top Mason, the whole thing a legacy of Mazzini, Master Mason and master intriguer.

It is no wonder then, that Mussolini outlawed Masonry in Italy in 1922 and exiled some of its leaders, such as Bartelemeo Torregiani. As usual, they went to London, the world capital for subversives and rebellious movements of every stripe, where the British press made an attempt to deceive the British people by reporting that the Italian Freemasons were "not welcome," to quote a leading newspaper, which published the story in 1931.

Already mentioned, the so-called Spanish Civil War was an attempt to install a Communist government and overthrow the Catholic Church of Spain. It was another Mason plot from whatever angle one looked at it. The Masons used the civil unrest their forces had stirred up, launching a furious and bloody assault on the Catholic Church. Official statistics show 50,000 nuns and priests lost their lives in the most cruel and inhuman fashion. So violent was its hatred for the Catholic Church, that in one terrible action, Socialist troops dug up the corpses of nuns and priests and then lined them up in sitting positions against the walls of a church, put crosses in their hands, and berated, denounced and cursed the dead with every vile invective they could muster.

Since the Western jackal press then, as now is in the hands of Freemasonry, the "loyalists" (the Communists, whose only loyalty was to Lucifer) received worldwide press support. While studying at the British Museum, I did a thorough reading of press coverage of war, and saw also a number of "newsreels" and documentary movies on the subject, especially some "newsreels" obviously the work of the Tavistock Institute.

Without exception, praise, adulation, support and comfort were heaped on the enemies of all mankind, while the forces of Christian Spain under Christian General Franco were subjected to every possible slander, calumny and unfounded accusations of brutality, which our jackal press in the West is so good at putting together and carrying out. I venture to suggest that had Christ Himself led the forces of Christian Spain, the jackals of the press would have somehow managed to undermine even His efforts!

CHAPTER 8

MASONIC ASSASSINATION'S OF WORLD LEADERS

The Masonic plot to assassinate Archduke Ferdinand at Sarajevo was successful, and World War I, with its terrible toll of white Christians was the result. Both WWI and WWII came about as a result of Freemason intriguing, plotting and planning.

I have already mentioned the assassinations of U.S. Presidents Lincoln, Garfield, McKinley and Kennedy. Assassinations carried out by Freemasons were not confined solely to U.S. presidents, they have covered a wide range of notable figures in history.

There are many other victims of Mason assassins, like Rep. L. McFadden, Chairman of the House Banking Committee, who attempted to put an end to the privately-owned "Federal Reserve Bank." It is neither federal nor a reserve bank, but an instrument of enslavement controlled by Freemasonry.

Certainly it is common knowledge that Paul Warburg, a 33rd Degree Mason who came from Germany, was the framer of the articles that successfully subverted the U.S. Constitution by establishing the Federal Reserve Banks in 1913. Masons in the U.S. Senate ensured its passage into "law."

Only two of the conspirators who left Hoboken in the sealed private railroad car on the 22nd of November 1910, bound for Jekyll Island off the coast of Georgia to plot and plan the Federal Reserve Banks, were not Freemasons. There is little reference to this conspiracy to subvert the Constitution in any official records. Not even Colonel Mandel House (a leading Freemason, who was the controller of President Wilson, who signed the Federal Reserve Act into law) mentions it.

As usual, where the vital interests of the American people are at stake, the jackal press, such as the New York Times, does not see fit to inform the American people of these vile acts of betrayal. Why was 1913 significant? Because without the Federal Reserve Banks it would not have been possible for Freemasonry to prosecute the First World War! In this war, and in the Second World War, the munitions factories belonging to international banksters (word for bankers and gangsters) were never touched! The Federal Reserve Bank's "elastic" currency provided the money for the arms trade, so you can rest assured, that nobody on either side of the conflict would have been foolish enough to destroy the assets of the bankers, that is, their arms and munitions factories.

It is my feeling that the real "internationalists" are the Western country's arms merchants. These men working under Masonic direction have two objectives: To create and prolong wars and to disturb peace through international terrorism. Then, to exploit the wars they expect will follow. Banks know no national boundaries and owe no allegiance to any country. Their God is Lucifer.

If possible, obtain a copy of Arms and the Men, a small

book published by Fortune Magazine and read it carefully. You will then have a clear picture of who is behind international terrorism, and perhaps more important, proof Freemasonry is the demon force loose in the world today, responsible for the Red Brigades (successor to the Mason terrorist group La Roja—The Reds) and the many hundreds of organized terrorist groups on the rampage throughout the world!

Another of Freemasonry's greatest successes and achievements is the artificially induced used of drugs and the lightning proliferation of the "trade" across the entire Western world. The role of China (principal supplier of raw opium) in the Vietnam conflict was to get American troops hooked on opium so that they would take their habit back to America with them. In this, China was successful. Statistics show, that 15% of America's military forces in Vietnam became addicted to heroin! The kingpins in the dope trade are top Freemasons.

If you find that hard to believe, then let me remind you of the greatest opium pushers the world has ever known; the British Government. The official British Government Opium Policy for China produced millions of addicts smoking opium. Lord Palmerston, a 33rd Degree Scottish Rite Freemason was in charge of this insidious trade. Profits from this satanic enterprise funded at least one major war on Christ—the Anglo Boer War (1899–1902.)

What happened to Princess Grace of Monaco? Her car is still under wraps in the police yard in Monaco. No one is allowed to inspect it. And why? Because Grace was murdered by the men of the P2 Freemasonic Order (the most secret branch of Italian Masonry) as a warning to her husband not to skim the profits of its dope operations in

Columbia and Bolivia!

The lawlessness of the U.S. Supreme Court is Mason-inspired. The lawless Supreme Court gave America abortion, a polite word for the wholesale murder of at least 50 million innocent babies, helpless and unable to protect themselves! May Almighty God forgive us for permitting Lucifer to murder the unborn.

King Herod was an infamous child-murderer, but abortion mills make him look saintly by comparison. Are the judges in favor of abortions that warm the benches of the Supreme Court any better than Herod? The lawlessness of the Supreme Court in banishing prayers from our schools is another triumph of Masonry. Lucifer is the very embodiment of lawlessness, and the Mason-controlled U.S. Supreme Court is carrying out his lawless program in the U.S. today.

I will ascend above the heights of clouds; I will be like the most High. (Isaiah Chapter II, vs. 14)

That is what the U.S. Supreme Court has done. It has set itself above the two greatest documents ever written, the Bible and the U.S. Constitution! Until we remedy this terrible situation, the United States will continue to drift down and down, and will eventually fall like a ripe plum into the hands of the worldwide conspiracy controlled by Lucifer, what we call Freemasonry. In the Book of Genesis, Ch.3 vs. 15, we read, that God has declared war on Lucifer. That conflict is going on right now. What are we doing about it?

Are we spending our time being anesthetized by spectator

sport on television, or are we doing our part to warn our fellow Americans that the fall of this great nation is imminent? Unless we arouse ourselves from the state of blind torpor and join God's war on Lucifer, we are of little value as soldiers of Christ.

Jesus said Cain was the first earthly outlaw. The Freemason movement honors Cain with its password, Tubal Cain. Masonry cannot co-exist with Christianity. Either Freemasonry will triumph or Christianity will smash it. The murder of Christ was the most lawless act ever carried out in the Universe, yet Masonry applauds it. One of its leading lights, Prudhon said:

> God is cowardice, folly, tyrannical, evil. For me then, Lucifer, Satan!

Communism is a Mason plot to further the kingdom of Lucifer in defiance of God's plan for his people on Earth. When we realize these things, many parts of the puzzle will begin to fall

into place. The kind of education we receive in our schools and universities will not equip us to combat these evils, because the knowledge of these things is deliberately concealed from us by our education controllers.

You won't find anything in our universities about the Federal Reserve Bank being an illegal, privately owned entity. Nor will you find anything about the secret government of the United States, the Committee of 300 and its Council on Foreign Relations, which is betraying and delivering this great nation into the hands of a One World Government-New World Order. This is a

Freemason plan, part of their universal effort to utterly destroy Christianity and wipe it off the face of the Earth.

This is the ultimate act of lawlessness. Remember Christ came to set us free from the Babylonian Law, upon which Freemasonry is based. Christ said that Satan is an outlaw, because he came to the Earth illegally, that is without a body. This is the reason why Christ had to be born of a woman, so He could legally be on Earth.

Only those who have a body are legally on Earth. Satan entered this world through the backdoor. (Christ said in the parables that he climbed over the wall.) Because of Satan, whom Masons adore, the United States has fallen into a desperate condition. Perhaps you are a Mason in the lower Degrees, and you say: "Now wait a minute. I have been a Mason for years and nothing like that ever happens in our Lodge."

To you and others like you, let me say, "You have been deceived." The vast majority of Masons are never told what goes on in the 33rd Degree.

As Eckert said:

> I have said, and I repeat that many Masons, even in the Masonic Degrees, do not suspect the hidden meaning of the symbols, which they use for what is taught and practiced in the highest Degrees.

Another authority on Masonry, Dom Benoit stated:

> The Reformed Palladium Rite has as a fundamental practice and purpose, the adoration of Lucifer, and it is

full of impieties and all the infamies of black magic.

Having been established in the United States, it has invaded Europe and each year it is making terrifying progress. All its ceremonial is full, as may well be imagined, of blasphemies against God and against our Lord Jesus Christ.

Need anything more to be said?

CHAPTER 9

PREVIOUSLY OVERLOOKED FACTS

The one thing we cannot overlook about Freemasonry is that it is a subversive movement. Masonry is many things to many people, but the common thread running through the history of Freemasonry is its enduring characteristic of secrecy for their security. All secret societies are subversive, some are also occult and political, but these facts are concealed from the main body of Masons, who seldom progress beyond the Fourth Degree.

Masonry is an organization that loves secrecy, and hates those who seek to expose its inherent evil. It has a fetish with secrecy. Masonry needs much light cast upon it. An open house would be suicidal for the movement. The purpose of this work is to throw some light on Masonry, so interfaced with the Jesuits and the Black Nobility, that it would be impossible to discuss Masonry in isolation, and without making some references to its co- conspirators.

This will become apparent as I proceed with the book. The so— called Mason creed is rather well described by Leo Tolstoy, who though not a Mason gave a clear account, shaded by a little too much sympathy toward Freemasonry and some of its principles.

Tolstoy details with "brotherhood" (the cornerstone of

Masonry, the Dluminati and Communism) as follows:

> Only by laying stone upon stone with the co-operation
> of all the millions of generations from our forefather
> Adam to our own times is the Temple reared, which is
> to be a worthy dwelling place of the great God.

He does not tell us that the letter "G" a symbol of Masonry
stands for Gnosticism, not God. Tolstoy goes on to say:

> The first and chief object of our Order, the foundation
> on which it rests and which no human power can
> destroy, is the preservation and handing down to us
> from the remotest ages, even from the first man—a
> mystery on which perhaps the fate of mankind
> depends. But since this mystery is of such a nature, that
> nobody can know or use it unless he be prepared by
> long and diligent self-purification, not every one can
> hope to attain it quickly, hence we have a secondary
> aim: that of preparing our members as much as possible
> to reform their hearts, to purify and enlighten their
> minds, by means handed on to us by tradition.

This is precisely the aims of the Illuminati and also those
of many other secret societies such as the Rosicrucians and
the Jesuits. The Black Nobility believes that they were
somehow endowed with special knowledge and chosen to
rule "from the time of Antiquity."

Thus can be seen the common denominators between
Masonry and other occult secret societies, with which the
world is presently so heavily infested. That Masonry is
entirely a dark lie can be deduced from the words of Christ,
who said ... that men love darkness (secret places) rather

than light, because their deeds are evil.

It is the notion of a longstanding tradition of fundamental importance that provides Masonry with motivation. All secret orders, even the Egyptian priesthood, were held together and given power and authority on the presumption that they knew secret things the common people did not know. Tolstoy again:

The third aim is the regeneration of mankind.

This involves the Seven Steps of Solomon's Temple. At this point I will mention that Solomon was probably the greatest magician who has ever lived. In modern times, a young Roma, born and living in the U.S. who called himself David Copperfield, achieved fame as a great magician. Roma gypsies have long been known as the practitioners of magic tricks, and Copperfield rose to great heights before his carrier was brought down by his arrest for rape. Because I believe, as also states in the Old Testament, that Christianity does not rest upon a foundation of magic, I am inclined to disregard the wisdom of Solomon as having little bearing on the teachings of Christ. My personal view is that Christianity is not fully dependent upon the Old Testament. Christianity really began with the Christ of Galilee. Christ was not of Jerusalem, not of Solomon and not of the Davidic line. Therefore Christians must reject out of hand as propaganda the idea that Masonry is based upon Christianity, because it speaks so much of Solomon.

If we make a study of this point, we shall have a better understanding both of Masonry and Christianity. My personal view is that Christ originally confined His ministry to Galilee, but was persuaded by His Disciples, to undertake a missionary crusade to Jerusalem. It was not long after his missionary trip to that city, that the Sanhedrin sentenced Him to be crucified. I do not believe that Solomon's magic tricks have any relationship to Christianity, any more than does Freemasonry. I wonder how many of us have ever stopped to question the close links between Freemasons and temples.

The Seven Steps of Solomon's Temple allegedly signify:

- ❖ Discretion
- ❖ Obedience
- ❖ Morality
- ❖ Love of mankind
- ❖ Courage
- ❖ Generosity
- ❖ Love
- ❖ Death

Once again I draw your attention to the upsurge in funeral scenes in almost every Hollywood and TV movie over the past 20 years. I point out to you, that the objective is to instill in all of us, a careless attitude toward death, which is in direct opposition to the teaching of Christ, who said, that death is the last enemy to be overcome. When we begin to think of death as a mere nothing, civilization is in danger of regressing back into barbarity.

By accustoming us to a casual acceptance of death, our sensitivities (it is hoped) will be blunted—the normal conscious horror of mass-killings will eventually give way to a sense of unconcern. I submit to you, that we are all being steadily brainwashed. Remember this point when you next see a movie which includes the almost mandatory grave-side funeral scene. The intention is to breed disrespect for the individuality of each one of us. We are not a mass of people, we are individuals.

A casual acceptance of death is against the teachings of Christ, and conforms to Freemason doctrines, as well as the doctrines of a large number of other secret societies decidedly Satanic in character and purpose. Frank King, the author of a notable book on Cagliostro, the Freemason, who is believed to have "discovered" the Egyptian Rite of Masonry, says that the initiation ceremony undergone by Cagliostro "was very similar to that which is performed in Masonic Lodges today." It includes several harmless but undignified scenes, which were intended to impress the candidate.

The initiate is hauled to the ceiling and allowed to dangle, signifying his helpless without divine aid. He was stabbed with a dagger, the blade of which collapsed into its handle to emphasize the fate which would be his should he ever betray the secrets of the Order. He had to kneel, divested of his clothing, to show his subservience to the Master of the Lodge. Cagliostro, a great magician, while on a visit to London, came across a book on Egyptian Rite. The book is by George Gaston. It so impressed Cagliostro that he began to promote it, calling it "The Egyptian Rite of Freemasonry," claiming it as his own. Cagliostro said that the Egyptian Rite was more solemn and ancient that regular Masonry. He promoted his "discovery" as a "higher Order of Masonry," open only to Masons above the 25th Degree. Like the original author, Gaston, Cagliostro claimed that the founders of the Egyptian Rite were Elijah and Enoch, and like them, members of the Egyptian Rite Masonic Order would never die, but be "transported" after death, each time rising from the ashes to live twelve lives.

There is little doubt, that "purified" Masons found the prospect of not having to die and being invested with twelve lives very pleasing, so there were a number of converts to Cagliostro's new, or should I say, ancient Order, notably Marshall Von der Recke and Countess Von der Recke of the Black Nobility, whose families are traceable to the Venetian Black Guelphs. The extraordinary Cagliostro, master magician and the "Solomon" of his day, was admitted to the Esperence Lodge of Freemasons Kings Head in London in 1776. After 14 months in London, he set off to promote his "new" Rite in Rome under the nose of his Catholic enemies and was promptly arrested by the Pope. If we knew nothing more than this of Freemasonry, it would already be clear that Freemasonry is the direct descendant of the Orphic and Pythagorean Cults, and has nothing whatever to do with Christianity, less still with the worship of God, which, as I have said, Masonry does not tell us while proudly claiming that the letter "G" stands for God. If Masonry were based upon Christianity, it would not hate with such fury and violence the Catholic Church.

CHAPTER 10

THE CATHOLIC CHURCH: ARCH-ENEMY OF FREEMASONRY

From the earliest days of its history the Catholic Church denounced Masonry as inherently evil. The Protestant Church on the other hand, and more particularly its Anglican branch, has not only openly tolerated Masonry, but in a number of cases some of the Anglican Church hierarchy holds high offices in Freemasonry. There are many instances, where Anglican priests control the most secretive and important Lodges, notably the Quator Coronati Lodge in London, and the notorious Nine Sisters Lodge in the 15th Arrondissment in Paris. Freemasonry has most scornfully declared that it has no fear of Protestantism, regarding it as the bastard offspring of Catholicism, its deadly and formidable enemy.

The Protestant Church cannot offer effectual opposition to the spread of Freemasonry. Freemasonry teaches as fact that masonry is the only viable alternative to Catholicism, which Mazzini (a leading Mason who played such a decisive role in bringing about the American Civil War) denounced with the utmost ferocity. It is perfectly correct to say that Freemasonry simply ignores the Protestant Church.

A 33rd Degree Mason told me:

We are the leading religion in the world today. We are older and wiser than the Catholic Church, which is why it hates us so much. The man who joins us feels that he is a member of a fundamental secret society religion, guarding the most ancient mysteries of life forces and the universe. We do not have the problem that organized religion encounters, namely how to inspire its followers with the profound sense of purpose, which we instill in our members. Look at the Catholics in Africa and South America. Would you say that they are imbued with a profound sense of purpose, of belonging?

Of course my Mason friend did not bother to explain that Freemasonry is based on deception, its true purpose being the worship of Lucifer. Continuing with his efforts to propagandize me (he was actually setting me up for proposed membership of his Lodge), he said:

The initiate we accept comes out with a sense of a neat and orderly universe, where his own aims and purposes are suddenly clearly defined. A tradition dating back to Adam stands behind him. The notion of brotherhood of man gives him a new sense of belonging to the human race. What is more, the world is full of benevolent brother Masons, who will not allow him to sink. This is of course an important attraction the Christian Church misses completely. Until the Christian Church learns to care about people, about each other in practical everyday terms, Christianity will continue to fade.

There is no doubt that a strong desire, a craving exists in all of us to have our physical needs met. Security is all-important, and my Mason friend certainly has a valid point. While Billy Graham and his fellow "televangelists" obviously take excellent care of their own needs, the rank and file members of their ministries are not at all cared for in the physical sense. There is a total lack of Christian brotherly love and concern for each other among Christians. No one can deny that such a glaringly obvious flaw exists and that it is a serious problem. In this we could take a leaf out of Masonry who takes good care of their members. No matter what the incestuous relationship is between Masonry, the Black Nobility and the Jesuits, their common burning desire and aim is the overthrow of existing order and to destroy Christianity. Whether we are Catholic or Protestant, it is our duty to oppose their goal with all our strength. All great conspiracies are cemented and bound together, energized by powerful ideological motives—in the case of Masonry, a common hatred of Christianity. We can include in their "hate list" the hatred of Republican ideals and nation states.

What do the conspirators have in common, apart from the foregoing? The answer is that they are backed one hundred percent by the immense wealth of "old families" and even foolishly by some royalty. In America they receive full support from the CFR, a descendent of the Essex Junto, one of the conspiratorial bodies that were behind the Civil War, which almost succeeded in breaking up the Union with the help of the wealthiest Boston families. The descendants of the oldest and most respectable families of Boston are continuing the work of the Essex Junto, trying to smash the U.S.—and they are backed by some of the richest banking dynasties in the world.

This clutch of traitors has an ally in the Vatican, one Clarissa McNair, who used to broadcast anti-American propaganda over the Vatican Radio. She was protected by a number of important Freemasons so that she managed to survive the wrath of the Pope.

The destabilizing of Poland, which laid the groundwork for the intended invasion, was carried out by Jesuit trained Freemason Zbigniew Brzezinski who "created" "Solidarity," the fake labor union, solely as a base to destabilize the government of General Jaruzelski. The Pope explained that he, Lech Walesa, was merely a tool in the hands of greater forces. After their meeting Walesa faded from the political scene. With one or two exceptions, most Popes were enemies of Freemasonry and consistently opposed the Jesuits. Pope John Paul II caused consternation in the Jesuit circles by appointing anti-Jesuit Paola Dezzi as head of the Order. "I will bring order to the Order," said the Pope.

The above cases, Poland and opposition to the Jesuits, are but two of a number of instances in which Popes were involved in running battles with Masonry. Very few people know anything about Pope John Paul's diplomatic efforts—such as his repeated warnings to America to drop its blinkered pro-Israel approach to Middle East politics, an attitude which the Pope believes will lead to the Third World War.

Poland is not the only case of deliberate treachery inside Western government since the Second World War. I recall that it was a certain Klugman, who inducted the traitors, British MI6 agents by the name of Burgess, McLean and Philby, into the service of the KGB. Philby, a life-long Freemason, got his job with the SIS (Special Intelligence Service) through Scottish Rite Mason and one-time Director of the SIS, Sir Stuart Menzies. Anthony Blunt, keeper of the Queens Pictures and spy extraordinary, began his career of treachery after joining the Masons.

Throughout his career, Blunt was protected by senior men in the SIS, fellow Masons, who like Blunt were devoted to the cause of Masonry. The SIS is riddled with KGB-Mason moles. Another scandalous fact is that Scotland Yard is run from the top down by Freemasons of the Scottish Rite. Masonry uses subtle methods of control. In the earlier days of its history, it was not always thus. It was more prone to use naked force to obtain its objectives than it does now. One truly remarkable example of what I am talking about concerns Cagliostro, whom I previously mentioned. Cagliostro was being tried on a charge of theft when the court proceedings were interrupted by a Sicilian marquis, a 33rd Degree Mason, leaping on the prosecutor and beating him to the ground. The charges against Cagliostro were quickly dropped. This account was verified by the Mason authority W.R.H. Towbridge and by Goethe. Today, Black Nobility-Mason Jesuits don't use direct force except as a warning lesson to errant members, as we note from the Roberto Calvi ritual hanging and the death of Grace Kelly. Calvi was the director of Banco Ambrosiano, who was guilty of skimming several millions of Mason money. He fled to England to seek protection from friends of his, only to walk into a fatal trap. He was hanged by Masons in their ritual fashion. When the occasion demands, Masons do not recoil from violence. The bloody oaths taken with each degree are brutal and repugnant.

Author John Robinson says in his book Born in Blood:

... To have one's tongue torn out by the roots, heart plucked from the breast, body cut in two with entrails burned to ashes appears to be overkill, literally, and is against the law of any land where Freemasons function, as well as bring against all religions whom the Masons welcome into the brotherhood.

John Quincy Adams who served as the sixth president of the United States was particularly and vehemently opposed to Freemasonry.

As Robinson says in his book:

Adams never missed an opportunity to condemn Freemasonry. He appealed to all Freemasons to abandon the order and to help abolish it for once and for all as it was totally incompatible with a Christian democracy. He wrote so many letters against Masonry that they can and do fill a book. In a letter to his friend Edward Ingersoll dated September 22, 1831, the ex-president summed up his attitude toward the Masonic oaths and their impact on the brotherhood.

There is a great deal of contention among historians and scholars of Masonry and the U.S. Constitution, in that the claims of Masonry having taken hold among the Founding Fathers remained firmly embedded in the new young Republic. The final draft of the Constitution came from many minds, but it was held that Freemasons were responsible for most of it.

This cannot be borne out, as Thomas Jefferson whose prose formed the better part of the document was strongly opposed to Freemasonry. Other leading writers were George Washington, Benjamin Franklin and John Adams. Although not a Mason, Adams is said to have agreed with Washington and Franklin. Jefferson remained the odd man out. But as it did with Cagliostro, Masonry still takes care of its own.

The "miraculous escape" from a maximum-security Swiss prison by Italian P2 Freemason Lucio Gelli attests to this and to Mason power. Gelli is living in Spain, unbothered by either the Swiss police or Reinhart Heydrich's hangover, Interpol. The odd thing about Gelli is that throughout the Second World War, he worked very closely with Mussolini, yet Mussolini was opposed to Freemasonry.

Perhaps it had to do with the fact, that when he was 17 years old, Gelli volunteered for an expeditionary force raised by Mussolini and sent to fight the Communists in Spain.

Later he joined the CIA. In March 1981, police raided Gelli's residence and discovered numerous documents showing that he had worked with Roberto Calvi of the so-called "Vatican Bank, " in other words, with the Mafia. Cardinal Casaroli later declared that the Vatican Bank had been robbed of millions of dollars.

CHAPTER 11

INTERPOL'S MASON CONNECTIONS

I used to wonder why it is that western nations make use of Interpol, a former Nazi apparatus, while condemning Germany for defending itself in the Second World War, until I discovered that Interpol is a Freemason network of spies, the private preserve of Masons, Jesuits and the Black Nobility. David Rockefeller makes extensive use of Interpol, which he literally bought lock, stock and barrel from Germany in the post war years, to keep a watchful eye on American right wing groups that might pose a threat to the Council on Foreign Relations (CFR).

The history which I have studied, not to be found in your regular history books, reveals that the Scottish Rite has always, and still does, provided leadership for many secret societies that infest the world. The Scottish Rite of Freemasonry began as the Mobeds Cult, sometimes called the Magi. Simon, the magician, known as Simon Magus, was a member of the Mobeds. It was Simon Magus who raised-up the cult of Gnosticism as an anti-Christian force, which he then took to Rome to counter the activities of St. Peter and Philo of Alexandria.

From Gnosticism grew the wellspring of hatred of Christianity, nation, states and republican ideals, eventually being distilled into the leader of all secret societies, which we know as Freemasonry. At the heart of Freemasonry lies the Scottish Rite in which Lucifer is edified and worshipped in the higher Degrees. British aristocracy imposed it on America with disastrous consequences for the young Republic. Britain is governed by the iniquitous Scottish Rite, heirs of John Ruskin's pre-Raphaelite Brotherhood of occultist-Templers and Isis Osiris cults. The Rosicrucians were a creation of Jesuits Robert Fludd and Thomas Hobbes, secretary to secret service agent Bacon and was the founding body of the Scottish Rite.

The creation of the Scottish Rite of Freemasonry was supervised by Sir William Petty, grandfather of the notorious Earl of Shelburne, orchestrator of the Swiss oligarchy led, London controlled bloody revolution we know as the French Revolution. The Jesuit placed Robert Bruce on the throne of Scotland, and made him head of the Scottish Rite. In on the conspiracy were the Cecils, who have dominated the rulers of England since the days of Queen Elizabeth I. The Cecils are directly related to the Venetian Black Nobility House of Guelph. For full details of the Cecils, please obtain a copy of my monograph, King Makers, King Breakers: The Cecils.

The secret history of Republican America is filled with the names of noted Scottish Rite traitors opposed to the young Republic. Albert Gallatin, a Swiss Black Nobility spy, Albert Pike, a degenerate, dissolute American, and Anthony Merry, the new British ambassador sent to the U.S. in 1804 by the Scottish Rite Mason, Prime Minister of England William Pitt, conspired with Timothy Pickering, Senator James Hillhouse and William Plummer to get New Hampshire to secede from the Union. Merry passed himself off as an inexperienced diplomat, but in reality he was an experienced Mason operative also involved in similar secessionist plots in New Jersey, Pennsylvania and New York.

William Eustas was the candidate the Scottish Rite put up to defeat the bid of John Quincy Adams for a Congressional seat. Freemasons made no secret of their complicity in the victory of Eustas over Adams. Years before, another Mason, Grenville, pushed through the Stamp Act.

The Mason-controlled British Parliament activated Henry VIII's statute, which permitted the British to bring to England, anyone from the American colony who was determined to remove the young country from the yoke of King George III, even if it meant going to war to do so.

The Scottish Rite Mother Lodge of the World, established in Charleston, South Carolina, by the hated oligarchy enemies of the young Republic, had as one of its chief messengers, a certain Moses Hayes, a Tory businessman, who traveled between all the states, carrying Scottish Rite directives and messages. Hayes refused to take the oath of allegiance when the war broke out. The high and mighty First National Bank of Boston was founded by Hayes, Arthur Hayes Sulzberger and John Lowell, under the name "Bank of Massachusetts." The Sulzbergers went on to run the New York Times as its nominal, although not actual owners. The New York Times' long and vile record of anti-Americanism is too well known to be dwelt upon here.

Active serious treachery planned by the Scottish Rite,

began in earnest in America with a patent given to Augustine Prevost, a member of the Swiss Black nobility enemy of the Republic, who held the Masonic title "Prince of the Royal Secret." All through our history, the Swiss and Venetian Black Nobility played us false, doing everything they could to undermine and destroy the young nation, which they saw as a threat to the old European order. The Lombard family, brought low and almost bankrupted in the 14th century were helped back up by "benevolent Masons," notably the Black Nobility Mason, Count Viterbos of Venice.

The Viterbos and Lombard families revived the power and prestige of Venice, and the Lombard banking dynasty has for hundreds of years continued to battle Republican America. The Viterbos revived Venice by conquering the Leventine/Byzantine Ottoman Empire, which was then parceled out between them and their family friends. The Venitian Black Nobility family Lonedon arranged the "conversion" of Ignatious Loyola, who suddenly repented of his ways and founded the Jesuit Order. The Jesuits were and are an intelligence gathering organization of Freemasonry, the Black Nobility, the Pallavicini, Contarini, Luccatto families and the American Eastern Liberal Establishment. It was the Jesuits who wrote the Catholic Bishop's pastoral letter condemning our nuclear deterrent as part of Masonry's 300 years of warfare against the Catholic Church and the USA.

One of Masonry's leading warriors was Vernon Walters, President Reagan's troubleshooter and ambassador to the UN. Walters was a prominent member of the Italian P2 Masonic Lodge. I wonder if President Reagan ever questioned Walters about his role on behalf of P2 in the Naxalite movement (1960– 1970). No less odorous than

JOHN COLEMAN

Walters was William Sullivan, who played a role in the overthrow of President Marcos of the Philippines. It was Sullivan, who asked Congress not to make overdue payments to the government of the Philippines for the rent of Clark Airfield and Subic Bay.

I notice that Sullivan did not ask Congress to suspend payments to Cuba for Guantanamo Naval Base, nor did Sullivan protest the flow of drugs out of Cuba. Sullivan made no mention of the biggest terrorist training camp in the Western hemisphere at that time located in Cuba, a facility that dwarfed training camps in Libya and Syria.

Both Walters and Sullivan were under the control of the ultra- secret Masonic Order, the "Order of Sion," which makes crucial decisions on behalf of Scottish Rite Supreme Council members operating inside various governments. Throughout our secret history, the evil force of Mason-Jesuits has dominated our decision-making apparatus, and this is certainly as true now as it was in the days of the American Revolution and the Civil War.

Reagan was totally in the grip of Masonry, acting out orders handed down by the CFR. There are a number of very important books on the Scottish Rite, of which several books are good sources of information:

At the top of my list are, The History of the Supreme Council, 33rd Degree, Northern Masonic Jurisdiction of the USA and its Antecedents, by Samuel Harrison Baynard; History of the Supreme Council, Southern Jurisdiction, 1801–1861 and Eleven Gentlemen from Charleston: Founders of the Supreme Council, mother Council of the World, both written by Ray Baker, and published by the

Ancient and Accepted Scottish Rite Supreme 33rd Degree Council at their own expense.

Baker was the accepted historian for the Scottish Rite in America, and according to him, the Scottish Rite was begun by Jewish merchants and Judaic religious leaders, who brought the patent from France in 1760, after which it was applied in Charleston and Philadelphia. Yet, according to other historians, Jews are not granted membership in the Scottish Rite. I find this very hard to believe, and I view it as a smokescreen around the question of who actually founded the Scottish Rite in the United States. King Solomon features prominently in Masonic rituals, and I know that he was of the Jewish religion as well as one of their great magicians. We also know that a great number of Masonic rituals are based on Solomon's magic rites.

CHAPTER 12

NOTED HISTORIAN
JOSEPHUS ON MASONRY

The noted Historian Josephus says, that a book of spells and incantations used in Mason rites was written by King Solomon. Also widely used in Masonry is the book, The Key of Solomon, which Josephus says Solomon wrote. Whatever the connection between the Scottish Rite and Judaism may or may not be, we do know that certain members of the British oligarchy adopted it as their own.

One of Masonry's prime movers in the U.S. was Augustine Prevost, whom we have already met, whose soldiers looted South Carolina during the American War of Independence. Prevost was Grand Master of the Lodge of Perfection, established by Francken, one of a group of Jewish merchants I mentioned a little while ago.

It was Francken, who passed the patent for the Scottish Rite to Augustine Prevost, who then ordered a fellow officer-Mason in the British Army to establish a lodge in Charleston. One of Augustine Prevost's relatives, a Colonel Marcus Prevost, was responsible for recruiting so called "Crown Loyalists " to fight against the Colonists.

Among the "Loyalists" were the antecedents of many of the Eastern Liberal Establishment, including those of the traitor McGeorge Bundy, one of the most active supporters of European oligarchy and royalty that we have on the political scene today, a man whose loyalties to the U.S. are very questionable. The Swiss Prevosts are perhaps not very well known because our history books do not say much about them.

Yet another Prevost, Sir George Prevost, was closely allied with Albert Gallatin, the Swiss-Mason spy sent to wreck America from the inside. Sir George commanded a British invasion force, which in 1812 sacked Washington and burned down the White house. No doubt the Bostonian "blue bloods" do not like to be reminded of British misdeeds, which could spoil the "special relationship" if too many Americans became aware of the record.

The Charleston Mother Lodge of the World gave the Scottish Rite patent back to France in 1804, Italy in 1805, Spain in 1809 and Belgium in 1817. One of the "Eleven Gentlemen from Charleston" was Frederick Dalcho, who held post in the Episcopalian Church in that city and was the leader of the "English Party" in South Carolina. Nothing much has changed since Dalcho's time—the American branch of the Church of England is riddled with Scottish Rite Masons.

Earlier I mentioned the claim that Jews are not admitted to the Scottish Rite. A notable Jewish Member of the Scottish Rite was John Jacob Astor, who began his Masonic career in New York, holding the post of Treasurer of the New York Grand Lodge. It was Astor who gave the 33rd Degree Mason traitor, Aaron Burr,

$42, 000. With this money, Burr was able to make good

his escape following the murder of Alexander Hamilton with the help of a Jewish Mason of high rank, John Slidell of New York.

Slidell moved to Charleston and New Orleans where he adopted the mannerisms of a Southern gentleman. He was closely associated with Aaron Burr. The two hatched a plot to take over Louisiana with the help of some New Orleans Jesuits, but the plot failed when it was discovered by patriots loyal to the U.S. At the time of his treacherous attempt to dismember the Union, Slidell held an important government position. He was supported by a whole clutch of fellow Masons. During his time there were hundreds of Masons inside the U.S. government. It is doubtful whether Vernon Walters and George Shallots find their Masonic oath compatible with the oath of loyalty to the U.S. As Christ said: "No man can serve two masters."

To those of you who believe in yoga, it is interesting that Freemasonry promotes it as a method of slowing down and stopping altogether currents of thought. Freemasonry does not like people to think. This piece of information was given to the Satanist, Alastair Crowley, by his protege, Alan Benoit, who got it from the noted Mason historian, Eckenstein.

Mason rituals below the Fourth Degree draw freely on the teaching of yoga, but in the Supreme Council of Masonry, yoga isn't taught or followed in any way. The Supreme Councils have some secrets of real interest to the normal world. It is known that Mazzini and Pike communicated by wireless telegraph long before Marconi "invented" it. Another startling secret held by the Elect of the Supreme Council is how to make silver and then turn it into gold.

This was demonstrated to Lord Palmerston (father of the Prime Minister of England) and 33rd Degree Mason Lord Onslow, by an Englishman named Price. Price said that he had received the secret formula "from the spirits." He proved his claim by fusing mercury with a white powder over a strong flame.

The mixture was tested by experts who found it to be pure silver. The silver was then melted over the flame and a reddish powder added to it. Several ingots were poured. Experts of both silver and gold who were present at all times, examined the new product very closely, and after on the spot testing, declared that it was indeed pure gold. The secret remains deeply hidden with the Elect of the Supreme Council of the Scottish Rite. As for Price, it is said, that he "committed suicide by drinking cyanide."

Was it really suicide, or was he poisoned? Did Price make a fatal mistake by proving his claim to Lord Palmerston as seems highly likely? The death of Price should surprise no one, for followers of Masonry have always been destroyers rather than creators.

The U.S. steel industry bears witness to this. Count Guido Colonna is not a well-known name in America. Few of the hundreds of thousands of unemployed steel workers will have heard of it. This Colonna is a Black Nobility Mason, who conspired with a member of the French Black Nobility, Count Davignon, to wreck the USA's steel industry. How well the conspiracy succeeded may be judged from the rusting, silent steel mills that dot the northern states. Who gave the order to proceed with the wrecking plan?

The answer is the Guelphs, better known as the House of Windsor. The Guelphs are the cornerstone of the oligarchy throughout the world.

If we are serious about halting the destruction of our industries, then we have to start at the top with the Guelphs, particularly the English Guelphs, who operate through the Scottish Rite of Freemasonry. The unique importance of this old family is totally overlooked in studies of "what's wrong with America's economy?"

The Windsors rule Britain and Canada, neither of which amount to anything more than their personal fiefdoms. The strength of the Windsors lies in their iron grip on the raw materials of the world and their awesome ability to strip countries of such raw materials. With a little research it becomes clear that they do this in Canada with timber, oil and furs.

In South Africa, it is gold and diamonds through the Oppenheimer Anglo American robbers; in Zimbabwe (former Rhodesia) it is chrome ore (the purest in the world) through Lonrho, a company belonging to a cousin of Elizabeth, Queen of England; and in Bolivia it is tin, through the Rio Tinto Company. (See The Committee of 300 for further details.)

The Windsor (Guelphs) do not care who holds political power in any country. Barring Russia, all office-holders are the same to them. They still keep their tight grip on the natural resources of most countries. Prince Philip directs the operations of various "ecological" groups, which are thinly disguised vehicles for keeping "outsiders" away from the raw material preserves of the Windsors. This "conservationist," president of the World Wildlife Fund, has no compunction about shooting 1000 pheasants over a weekend!

Through the Hambros Group, the Windsor's income runs into billions of dollars. The Hambros Group maintains it position of strength through a network of Mason stockbrokers. Other Mason-run companies are: Shearson, Amex, Bear Stearns and Goldman Sachs, all under the Hambros umbrella, which is ultimately controlled by the Black Venetian Windsor Guelphs.

The Guelphs have been associated with Masonry for hundreds of years. Their links with England began with the Venetian dynasty of Corso Donati in 1293.

CHAPTER 13

AMERICAN CIVIL WAR WAS THE WORK OF FREEMASONRY

From start to finish, the dreadful American Civil War was the work of Freemasonry. The Mason-run account of it does not appear in any of our history books for obvious reasons. The Anglophile Families, who did not join the Colonists in the war against Britain, moved to Nova Scotia, from where they assisted the British throughout the American Revolution. Later they returned to the U.S. and carried on the tradition of helping the British Freemason conspiracy against Republican America, which culminated in the Civil War.

In that cruel disaster America lost 500,000 men, more than our combined losses in both World Wars. The Civil War was a British-European oligarchic Freemason plot to split the country into warring states, and then walk in and take back what they lost in the American Revolution. In this they were ably supported by a nest of "American" traitors. The infamous Eastern Liberal Establishment might have succeeded and there would be no United States today had it not been for the outstanding work done by the American patriots Clay and Carey.

We must learn this lesson in history, even though such history does not appear in historian Charles Beard's work. Freemasonry never gave up after losing the war with the

Colonists. Things came to the head in 1812, after a long period in which the British Navy seized American ships and imprisoned thousands of American sailors. The Kissingers of the day said America could do nothing about it, and they were right. Swiss Masonry's mortal enemy, Albeit Gallatin, had gutted our defense budget, leaving us without a real navy. Smarting from two defeats at the hands of the young Republic in less than 150 years, the British again turned on the U.S. by selling their Derwent centrifugal flow jet engines to the USSR for installation in the MIG 15 fighter planes, which were used to bomb and strafe U.S. troops in Korea. Without the Derwent engine, it would have taken the Soviets at least fifteen years to build a jet fighter.

Just as today there are those of us who deeply distrust the "special relationship" between the U.S. and Britain, having seen what it has done to our country, so in the days of the Essex Junto, there were patriots who saw through British Masonry's plotting and planning. They tried to expose the treachery of Caleb Cushing and John Slidell.

They warned against the "free trade" economic policies of the day, the very same policies we permitted Milton Friedman to sell to the "conservative" Reagan administration.

Free trade is a British Freemason concocted plot to destroy our economy. It is time that we took the lid off the history of the Venetian Black Nobility related Scottish Rite traitors like the pirates Sam and George Cabot and the Pickerings, who made their fortune out of the twin miseries of opium and slave trading.

McGeorge Bundy's antecedents were slave traders. It was Freemason John Jacob Astor who permitted the Pickerings to get into the preposterously lucrative China opium trade. The truth must be told about the whole nest of vipers writhing around inside the British East India Company, Loring, Adam Smith and David Hume. It was Loring who stole the rations of Americans taken prisoner by the British during the American Revolution, which he then sold to the British Army for a huge profit, leaving the American prisoners to starve to death on terrible prison ships.

When I first read Mathew Carey's, The Olive Branch, I could not believe what I was reading. But over the years I found that everything that Carey claimed has very much been substantiated.

Another work that I recommend is The Famous Families of Massachusetts. These famous families have among their ranks the descendants of the Lorings, the Pickerings and the Cabots, descendants of the Masonic network originally set up in this country by the French oligarchist Cabots and the Swiss Prevosts.

Of such stuff is the Anglophile Eastern Liberal Establishment made. I could go on quoting family names and their history, which everything possible has been done to conceal. Their loyalties lie with the European and British royal families and oligarchies through the Scottish Rite of Freemasonry. They may be able to successfully deny their history, but that does not alter the proven fact that their strong connections with Masonic centers of intrigue has proved.

Today they have indirect contact with the Seven Sisters

Lodge in Paris. This Lodge runs a vast drug smuggling operation that reaches into the very heart of the "crowned cobras of Europe." They believe, like Robert Holzbach, the Scottish Rite head of Union Bank of Switzerland that "Sovereignty is no substitute for solvency."

In other words, money power transcends all considerations. Holzbach is typical of the money power that pitted the Old World against the young Republic of the U.S. Holzbach works closely with the Italian P2 Masonic Lodge, established to work for the return of the House of Savoy to the Italian throne. Through the Scottish Rite-P2 network, no one's privacy is secure. The U.S. government has its connections in these circles. Your numbered account in a Swiss bank may already be known to the U.S. Government or interested party for that matter. This is generally known, which is why those with money to hide, no longer bank in Switzerland.

Those who belong to the Episcopalian Church in America, please be advised that your Archbishop, Robert Runcie, is a member of the Supreme Council of the Scottish Rite of Freemasonry. If it were not so, then he would never have been "approved" as Archbishop by Elizabeth Guelph. Runcie is the personal contact man for Queen Elizabeth and the World Council of Churches.

The tremendous influence of the Scottish Rite on our past history and on important decisions, domestic and foreign, made by every U.S. administration, cannot be measured in terms of damage done to the best interest of the country. Just as it was responsible for planning the Civil War, so the Scottish Rite of Freemasonry is planning for the Third World War. Unless we take stock of what powerful forces are running U.S. affairs, no matter who occupies the White

House, we have no hope of combating the enemy. The only way we can thwart the plans of the Scottish Rite traitors is to expose their activities.

To do this, our patriots must be kept informed of what the Scottish Rite, and indeed, all Masonry stands for, viz., the overthrow of existing order and the destruction of nation states, especially those with republican constitutions, the destruction of the family and the destruction of Christianity. I found it most difficult to separate this message from the one I did on the influence of oligarchic and royal families on our affairs. I would recommend that you also obtain a copy of that work, King Makers and King Breakers: The Cecils, and use it in conjunction with this book on Freemasonry.

CHAPTER 14

CONSPIRACIES: THE ONE WORLD GOVERNMENT

On a subject as vast as the secret society known collectively as the Free Masonic Order and by various other names, it is not possible to deal with the origins of Freemasonry fully. Therefore, the object of this work is to provide material that will help you to better understand economic and political events now shaking the world by pointing out the connection between these destructive satanic events and Freemasonry. Please be patient, don't stop right here and write and tell me that you are a member of one or another of the many Masonic orders and that you know the Masons are a fine philanthropic society, which has banned political and religious matters from its discussions and deliberations.

The problem is that the lower degree Masons do not ever know what the highest degree Masons are doing. The very structural nature of the movement makes it impossible for them to know. Thus, it is a relatively easy matter for the top leadership to deceive the rank and file members as to the actions, aims and intentions of Masonry. And if by chance one of the members of the lower order should gravitate to the top, he is sworn to secrecy on pain of death never to reveal what he knows to the lower brethren or anyone else outside of the Masonic order. This oath of silence is very strictly enforced. I will try to avoid mentioning the many different religious cults and beliefs connected to Freemasonry and stay with the aspects of English and American Masonry.

English Masonry is said by most authorities on the subject, to have established itself in the year 1717 under the title Guilds of Operative or Working Masons, and it opened its doors to what was called Speculative Masons, that is, non-working Masons, thereby creating a combined movement called the English Grand Lodges. The older Guild Masons were in existence for many centuries before 1717, but they were not, I repeat, not a political force. They concerned themselves only with making their trade, craft and/or profession a closed shop; that is to say, they preserved their secrets against outsider penetration.

The early Masons, that is before 1717 had three degrees only—Entered Apprentice, Fellow Craft and Master Mason. When the amalgamation occurred, the Guild Masons allowed big changes to take place, the first being that the name of the Christian God was eliminated from the ritual, Blue Masonry, as it became known, was by that period a virtually new movement and it ended the cooperation with Craft Masons. In short, the non- working speculative Masons took over completely and the old order disappeared from the scene.

Out of the new order grew a new militant and revolutionary Masonic Order called The Scottish Rite. While barring Grand Orient rituals, that is the European Masonry, English Freemasonry has not barred the Scottish Rite and this revolutionary ritual has, like a deadly virus, taken over all Masonic cells in England and America to produce more of its own kind.

The greater part of the membership of English Masonry remains at the Third Level, generally unaware of the evils being perpetrated in its name in the higher degrees. By time the Ninth Degree is reached, the revolutionary nature of the Scottish Rite Masonry is exposed to qualifying candidates, that being its final purpose; subversion of the State by Masonry as taught in the 33rd Degree, which also explains why many 33rd Degree Masons have been in charge of dissolving existing governments in many countries.

For example, in the French and American Revolutions, the War Between the States and latterly in Zimbabwe where a 33rd Degree Mason, Lord Somas, betrayed Zimbabwe into the hands of a Communist tyrant, under the fraudulent guise of "majority rule" and the total sell out of South Africa by Masons in charge of Britain and the U.S.

Somas was one of those "determined men of Masonry" described by Disraeli, the Prime Minister of Britain and a Mason, when he discussed particularly the Scottish Rite and Grand Orient Lodges saying:

> We must take into account Secret Societies who can disconcert all measures at the last moment, who have agents everywhere, determined men encouraging assassinations, etc.

This certainly does not sound like the philanthropic society Masons claim it to be and, in truth, it is not. The question arises; why do we have to have secret societies anyway? America was founded on Christian principles which clearly state, "that men like darkness rather than light so that their evil deeds may be obscured." This, I believe, is the real reason for secret societies; basically their deeds are evil. There is no other explanation for the need of secrecy! There is no need to expound on the secret society which ran the French Revolution. By now all historians are agreed that it was the Masonic Jacobin Club.

Here is what a very notable Grand Master of the Supreme Council of Scottish Rites, Dominica Anger, had to say when confirming the 33rd Degree upon newly qualified Masons about to receive it:

> Brother thou have finished thy instruction as a chief of Freemasonry. Pronounce thy supreme oath. I swear to recognize no fatherland but that of the world. I swear to work hard everywhere and always to destroy frontiers, boundaries of all nations of all industries, no less than of all families. I swear to dedicate my life to the triumph of progress and universal unity and I declare to profess the negation of God and the negation of the Soul. And now Brother, that for thee, fatherland, religion and family have disappeared forever in the immensity of the work of Freemasonry, come to us and share with us the boundless authority, the infinite power that we hold over humanity. The only key to progress and happiness, the only rules of good are thy appetites and instincts.

That in a nutshell is the essence of what the Scottish Rite Freemason Order is all about and it is the Scottish Rite that dominates American Masonry. One of the most interesting things about Communism, Freemasonry and the Jesuits is that they all have a notable figure in history connecting them—Karl Marx, the man who claimed Weishaupt teachings as his original "manifesto."

Marx fiercely (and often violently) defended the Jesuits throughout his life. Marx is the connecting man. Marx also ardently supported the Freemason Secret Society, which is in my view a significant connection "overlooked" by nearly all historians. The overlooking is a deliberate process. That Socialism is being used to further the One World Government goal cannot be denied, and it is interesting to note that Marx, an avowed hater of religion, should so passionately espouse Jesuitism.

Ignatius Loyola founded the Jesuit Order on April 5, 1541, which was later sanctioned by Pope Paul XI. It has something of a Masonic flavor to it, in that it consists of six grades or degrees with the head of the Order being known by military rank, i.e., a General, who demands absolute unswerving loyalty from all Jesuits and he in turn takes absolute power in all matters over each and every Jesuit. The General has the power to admit openly or secretly, persons who are not members of the Society. Superiors and Rectors are required to report to the General each week on all persons with whom they have had dealings or connections. The Jesuits are a powerful counter force against the Pope, a force they have never hesitated to use as they did during the Inquisition, from which the Jesuits distanced themselves as far as possible. Popes have always viewed the Jesuits with suspicion, so much so that in 1773 the Order was banned. In defiance of the Pope, Frederic II of Prussia protected the Jesuits for his own purposes.

In case any reader should take exception to the connection made between the Jesuits and Freemasonry, let me say here that probably one of the best authorities on the matter is Heckethorn, and I am going to quote what he said:

There is considerable analogy between the Masonic and Jesuit degrees; and the Jesuits also tread down the shoe and bare the knee because Ignatius Loyola thus presented himself at Rome and asked for the confirmation of the order.

Not satisfied with confession, preaching and instruction, whereby they had acquired unexampled influence, they formed in Italy and France in 1563 several congregations, i.e., clandestine meetings in subterranean chapels and other secret places. The Segregationists had a sectarian organization with appropriate catechisms and manuals which had to be given up before death, wherefore very few copies remain.

The Jesuits sought to help the New World Order by strongly supporting such revolutionary persons as Karl Marx, who in turn fiercely defended the Jesuits as I said earlier. Other notables who defended Jesuitism and Freemasonry were Adam Smith, the British East India spymaster who was used to promote false economic theories, along with co-conspirator, Thomas Malthus. Both were protegees of Scottish Rite Mason, the Earl of Shelburne, who fomented the French Revolution and the American Revolution. Actually what all these men, including Marx, were defending was Feudalism, which was destroyed forever by the American Revolution.

Jeremy Bentham, a devil-worshipping Satanist in the class of Albeit Pike, opposed Republicanism, as do all Freemason-Jesuit conspirators today. The rentier families who ran the world during Bentham's time saw danger in the freedom of man through a republican form of government, so they set about using every means at their disposal to nullify the great benefits accruing from the American Revolution. That struggle with Freemasonry is still going on today in 2009, but it is now in its final phase. It is significant that the leaders of the One World Order conspiracy are predominantly Freemasons and in some cases, also Jesuits like Brzezinski, who is also an Aquarian. (A member of the Aquarian Conspiracy) They are in the vanguard of the struggle to overthrow the American Republic, which is such a hated thing in the eyes of the Black Nobility of Europe and the so-called aristocrats of America.

The Black Nobility families live in Italy (Venice, Genoa and Florence), Switzerland, Britain and Bavaria, and that is where its chief members are to be found and from whence all manner of crimes against humanity have since the 14th Century been plotted and carried out.

CHAPTER 15

AN INSIGHT INTO KARL MARX

Karl Marx was in fact a creation of one of these ancient oligarchies and proclaimed the Soviet Union as an oligarchy. These oligarchies included the United States and they declared republicanism a deadly enemy, which must be wiped out by all available methods.

Albeit Pike declared himself totally opposed to a republican system with democratic principles. One such method is through religious fanaticism, coupled with penetration of cults and religious orders. And it is not only a republican form of government they want to see destroyed. They wish to see the whole United States returned to a feudal system in which the "noble aristocrats" of the Eastern Establishment have full dictatorial powers.

I have not come across any writer in the U.S. "conspiracy culture" who has explained feudalism to my satisfaction. Those who have written about the subject only served to demonstrate their lack of knowledge of its true meaning. With this in mind I take leave to enlarge on feudalism as it has a direct connection with Masonry.

In the Dark Ages that ruled Europe for centuries, the individual was helpless. Preservation of life was the major factor and men pledged themselves in complete servitude to the strongest among them who in return would provide them protection from those who would prey upon them. The strong men pledged themselves to even stronger men, and out of this grew the feudal system. Men would pledge themselves to military service of the strongest group for given periods of time—say 50 days a year.

This led to the rise of a warrior class who became the nobility. They required armaments, horses and fortified places to afford protection which came through "free" labor. The fortified places grew from stockades to strong stone buildings, lofty in design and execution.

Stone cutters, masons, smiths and iron workers, all had to donate free labor to the building of these super-structures. The prime source of wealth was the land and the labor of those who worked on it to produce goods that translated into wealth. The serf's condition changed very little over many centuries, some gradually becoming tenant farmers while making payments to the manor lord. Neither he nor his family could marry without the permission of the manor lord which usually involved payment of a fee. He was never a free man.

The ever-present barrier to his freedom was the law that required him to remain where he was. In other words, he was not allowed to move. On death, his best farm animals went to the lord of the manor. Albert Pike and his fellow Masons promised "complete freedom" to all who would become members of Freemasonry.

Albeit Pike's closest friend and collaborator was Giuseppe Mazzini (1805–1872), the Italian Mason leader who could not tolerate the industrial capitalist system. Mazzini was a Satanist and also a Jesuit priest!

Mazzini was the founder of the Young Europe league, which very soon opened up a branch in America called Young America. Karl Marx was one of the earliest members of the radical Freemasonic Mazzini movements starting in 1840, so it is quite clear that Freemasonry created Karl Marx as a revolutionary figure championing the workers, in order to use him as a club to beat industrial capitalism to death. Mazzini, the Jesuit Freemason supporter, actually launched Karl Marx's career against capitalism by calling together notable Communist Masons and founding the radical "International Working Men's Association."

From then onwards, Karl Marx was seldom out of the public eye. Marx only developed his hatred of industrial capitalism following that fateful London meeting at which the International Working Man's League was founded, from which Marx emerged saying:

I am determined to smash all industrial capital political movements where I find them.

Marx also said:

All evil must be laid at the door of industrial capital development.

Marx never failed to preach this theme. I hope that you, the reader, can see just how much harm we have suffered because of the duplicity of Freemasonry and Jesuitism. Both movements remain at war with the U.S.

This was part of the announced intentions of high-degree Masons such as Pike and Mazzini; to overthrow the existing order which Weishaupt set out to do in 1776, and ordered the Illuminati to carry out. The word "imperialism" was invented at the International Working Men's Association and began to be used quite frequently from 1890 onwards. Because America became the greatest industrialized nation in the world and because of its amazing opportunity for growth, the United States became the most hated nation, more so because of its unique republican form of government. The oligarchy families in America did everything to support such a climate of hatred. So much of what Marx expressed as "ugly Americanism" gained ground around the world. Of course, no one thought of pointing out that Lenin's ideas were about as close as one could get to an imperialistic system; Communism being nothing but an oligarchy-based system of narrow capitalism. It was never true Communism and it isn't Communism now. It is simply put, brutalized capitalism with power, complete power, in the hands of a few men.

CHAPTER 16

LOOKING BACK IN HISTORY

When I was a young student, I read Tacitus's history of Augustus Caesar. I was filled with amazement. Surely, I thought, the people of Rome could see that they were being degraded and that Rome must soon vanish? Why didn't someone do something to halt Rome's downward slide? Why have we in America also failed to see that America is being degraded? Surely the people must see that the Eastern Liberal Establishment and its alliance with the British oligarchy are ruining this country?

Surely the people must see that we are in the final years of the most marvelous Republic the world has ever known? The answer is that the American people are no different from the Romans. They see nothing of the kind! Nor do they wish to be troubled by people like me who try to point this out. "Leave us alone," they say. "America is not ancient Rome. We have our Constitution. We are strong. We will not be defeated."

That is precisely the point. Because you, the American citizen have a Constitution, the Eastern Establishment regards you as a threat they must work night and day to eliminate. And what has happened to our Constitution, the greatest document after the Bible? It has been trampled underfoot and brushed aside!

I am going to say quite firmly that I was the only one to draw attention to the connection between the Malvinas War and the Eastern Establishment. I was also the first, and for a very long time, the only one to write about the Club of Rome, Felipe Gonzales, the Global 2000 Report and cultism, such as the New Age of Aquarius. Today these names are publicized in many right wing publications, but for nearly ten years, the only information on these names came from my archives.

The Malvinas War was a war fought and on behalf of the British Black Nobility and of Elizabeth Guelph, the Queen of England. America had no right to help those haters of real freedom to triumph over the Argentineans. Yet we supplied the British with every conceivable support in weapons and back-up systems. By doing so we fouled our own nest, ignoring that John Quincy Adams drafted the famous Monroe Doctrine to prevent just such an occurrence.

The Eastern Establishment ruling class, long associated with their British counterparts, in effect tore up their Monroe Doctrine by support of the British aggressors, saying in effect that they, with their hatred of our Republic, know what to do with documents like the Monroe Doctrine, and they did it during the Malvinas War, pouring contempt and ridicule upon its pages, over which "conservative" President Reagan, presided.

In pouring scorn on the Monroe Doctrine, the Eastern Establishment, enemy of the people of America and its great Republic, also repudiated the 1812 victory over the British by the small and inadequate American Navy. That great American naval victory came after Swiss-born traitor, Gallatin (Secretary of the Treasury), had done everything in his power to prevent an American Navy being built at all. Gallatin served the British, Swiss and Genoese Black Nobility and their rentier-banker families and did all he could to strangle and choke the young American Republic to death. Gallatin was the exact opposite of John Quincy Adams and Benjamin Franklin.

Whereas John Quincy Adams and Franklin served America, Gallatin served the old feudal families of Britain, Venice, Genoa and Austria in exactly the same way that President Wilson, House, Roosevelt Stimson, Knox, Bush and Clinton were to serve the conspirators, while they worked to overthrow the American Republic in favor of a despotic slave state One World Government.

To return to the War of 1812. Following the utmost savagery against its merchant fleet by British warships and their surrogates, the Barbary Coast pirates, America finally declared war on the British—but not the Eastern Establishment. The small American Navy eventually defeated the mighty British Navy. Finally, when peace came, the Treaty of Friendship, Navigation & Trade ceded to Spain and then to Argentina, the Malvinas Islands.

Thus the Argentines had legal title to the Malvinas Islands. Yet George Bush, George Shultz and Alexander Haig, servants of the Eastern Establishment, spurned the memory of those brave Americans who defeated the British for the second time and through their treachery in helping the British to invade the Malvinas, tore up the Monroe Doctrine and once again made the U.S. subservient to British and European feudalists. And it was President Reagan who presided over this desecration.

Yes, we excoriated the names of our hero-statesmen, John Quincy Adams and President Monroe. We not only acquiesced in permitting a belligerent British force into our hemisphere, we helped them to defeat a friendly nation with whom we had a treaty agreement. If there is anyone who still doesn't believe that the British are in control of America, I urge you to reconsider carefully, not only what they did to Argentina, but also what they did to our own country, the USA. Those responsible for violating the Monroe Doctrine ought to have been tried for treason and punished if found guilty.

They betrayed everything the Republic of the U.S. stood for when they let the British into our hemisphere! That is what it amounted to. Surely somebody could have seen what was happening? Surely someone could have stopped it? Are we as blind as the Romans were?

The answer in the second instance is that nobody in America, including our President, is strong enough to stop the Whore of Babylon, the Eastern Establishment money power, from doing exactly what its European masters order it to do! We are being borne along by a swift and rising tide, propelled along at a rapid pace towards the fatal day when we are to be submerged under a One World Government. There is no stopping that furiously on—rushing flood tide! Even those, like me, who have been writing for years on the subject and know exactly what is going on, can do little to stop the tragedy. Just as surely as Rome fell, America will fall.

We are entering the last few remaining years of our Republic. But few perceive it, even as Tacitus stated, neither Augustus Caesar nor anyone perceived that Rome was falling.

The chief architects of our decline are the Jesuit-Freemasons and their intertwined connections with the American Eastern Establishment and the British, Venetian-Genoese-Swiss Black Nobilities. Mrs. Thatcher's and Henry Kissinger's plot to betray America by their back-door secret deals with Moscow, proved it).

Just in case you feel that my belief in the existence of secret deals between the Eastern Establishment and the USSR are out of hand, let me tell you that one of the worst traitors in the history of the American republic, McGeorge Bundy, a so-called "blue blood " traitor, formed one of the premiere institutes of its kind, the International Institute for Applied Systems Analysis, in collaboration with KGB agent Alexei Dzhermen Gvishiani, who also just happened to be the son-in-law of the late Premier Alexei Kosygin (1904–1980). McGeorge Bundy strongly supports the fatal Malthusian Freemason doctrine, which today is killing the economies of the Western nations. McGeorge Bundy is a member of the Scottish Rite Order of Freemasons, as was Kosygin.

McGeorge Bundy played a prominent role in opposing all of America's efforts to gain nuclear parity with the Soviet Union, and along with the Pugwash conferees (Pugwash Conference on Disarmament) nearly all of whom were Freemasons, did inestimable harm to America's defense capabilities. Along with Kissinger, Bundy allied himself with the Pugwash SALT promoters which he knew would end in weakening America.

Both McGeorge Bundy and Kissinger sold out to the same Swiss, German, and British Black Nobility families who fought against Washington in the American Revolution and in the War of 1812, even as the Black Nobility Freemasons continue to fight the American Republic.

Where do McGeorge Bundy, Kissinger, Harriman, Rockefeller, Cabot, Lodge, Bush, Kirkland (the present labor leader, whose great-great grandfather fired the first shot at Fort Sumter to start the destruction of the Republic), the Lowell's, the Astor's and all of the Eastern Establishment families get their beliefs and anti-republicanism ideas?

That is fairly easy to answer—from the Earl of Shelburne, (William Petty 1737–1805) the head of British Secret Intelligence Service and a master spy and perhaps even more importantly, the head of the ultra-secret fanatic Scottish Rite Order of Freemasonry! In this connection, we see again the vital role played by Freemasonry in shaping not only the affairs of the sell out United States, but indeed the entire world as it moves towards a society called a One World Government.

Who was this master conspirator, this Shelburne, who ruled the hearts and minds and philosophies of those eminently respected "old money" families of Boston, Geneva, Lausanne, London, Genoa and Venice, grown unbelievably rich out of opium and slave trading: I refer to the William Pitt, Mallet and Schlumberger families. Shelburne certainly ruled the hearts and the minds of all of the Eastern Liberal Establishment and many, many other so-called prominent and influential families.

I first mentioned Lord Shelburne in my writings some twenty years ago. At that time, no right wing publication or author had ever referred to the autocratic British blue blood that ran the opposition to the American Revolution.

Shelburne was first and foremost a Scottish Rite Freemason with very strong links to Jesuits in England, France and Switzerland. He was not only the controller of William Pitt, British Prime Minister, but also the controller of the terrorists Danton and Marrat and Eastern Establishment traitors led by Aaron Burr, and Adam Smith, the British East India spy-turned-economist, and Malthus, upon whose tide of flawed concepts the economies of the West are being swept into perdition.

CHAPTER 17

FREEMASON LEADER SHELBURNE

L ord Shelburne was the man who did the most to destroy the benefits that mankind had received following the 15th Century Renaissance, and the man who did the most to betray the Christian ideals as Christ taught by Christ, our social, moral political ideals, and our concepts of individual freedom as embodied in the Constitution.

In short, Shelburne was the near history father of revolution, slavery and the New Dark Ages of a One World Order. Shelburne hated and detested the Renaissance. He was definitely a special interest believer who felt the common man is only on Earth to serve the upper class, Shelburne's class. He also detested industrial capitalism and was an ardent supporter of feudalism, a near perfect example for Karl Marx to follow.

Moreover, it was William Petty who founded the thrice-accursed London Royal Society, forerunner of the Royal Institution for International Affairs, controller of U.S. foreign affairs, the Council on Foreign Relations in New York. The London Royal Society and its progeny, the Royal Institute for International Affairs and the New York Council on Foreign Relations are both based on Freemason scholar, Robert Fludd's writings and on Jesuit-Rosicrucianism.

Other Freemasons who controlled the Royal Society were Elias Ashmole and Lord Acton, both very much in the top echelon of Mason leadership. These men, together and separately, controlled the actions of the British Prime Minister, William Pitt and John Stuart Mill, Lord Palmerston and later such men as H. G. Wells and John Ruskin (Ruskin the mentor of Cecil Rhodes and Lord Alfred Milner) as well as the Freemasons who ran the Jacobins of the French Revolution infamy.

It was Lord Milner who launched the savage Boer War, flinging the might of the British Army against the tiny Boer Republics. He, like Shelburne, hated republicanism. These notable Freemasons brought untold havoc, misery, pain and suffering, and economic chaos to all nations, but let us not forget that it was William Petty, Earl of Shelburne, whose teachings inspired them and made it all possible.

Let us not forget either that William Petty, the Earl of Shelburne, and I repeat this, was first and foremost a Freemason. Freemason rituals in the 33rd Degree teach there is no God, but talk a great deal about the ancient evil cults. Mesopotamia and Egypt were the lands where these evil cult-were practiced, and carried by the Earl of Shelburne to the West and on which today's Club of Rome and Aquarians are modeled, having existed since antiquity. They had no regard, no pity for a mother whose child was snatched away from her by the priests of Baal to be burned alive in the iron arms of Molok as a sacrifice to him.

Those "hunting and gathering societies," as they are known, are to be found in certain Freemason orders to this very day. And make no mistake about it, the cults are the very embodiment of all that is evil, cults like Dionysus, to which the mighty heads of Europe's royalty belong, Magna Mater, Isis, Astarte, the evil, vile Chaldean cult, and the Lucifer cult or the Lucifer Trust, lately called the Lucius Trust, to which Robert McNamara, Cyrus Vance and many of the Eastern Establishment notables belonged.

(Let me say, there are many other cults to which several high-rank Freemasons belong ~ those connected to the One World Government order—and I shall touch on these as I proceed.)

But before detailing what the Freemason cultists of modern times are doing to bring about a One World New Order-Age of Aquarius "Utopia," I want to go back to the historical Masonic figures of the American Revolution, the War between the States commonly known as the Civil War, and then continue on to more recent times.

I hope to show you that a red line of hatred for the American Republic has run through our history for more than 250 years, and which hatred is stronger today than ever before, as America enters its final phase before the twilight of the New Dark Ages settles into blackness over the Earth and all its remaining inhabitants.

Before going into some of these details, let me say that the hatred of Christianity is even stronger in 2008 than it was in the Middle Ages. It is worthy of mention that there is very little difference between the aims and objects of today's treacherous Eastern Establishment Freemasons and the policies of International Socialism. "Our" traitors have always cooperated with their counterparts in Venice. Indeed it was the "blue bloods" of America and those allied to the Black Guelph in Europe, particularly Lord

Alfred Milner the Scottish Rite Mason, who created Vladimir Lenin.

As I said earlier, the Bolshevik Revolution was not some obscure movement that succeeded in overthrowing and enslaving a major nation. Rather, it was the outcome of planning and plotting by Masons, which began in 1776 with the Jesuit—connected Adam Weishaupt's war against the Catholic Church. Not only did the plot to communize Russia come from the West, but also the vast fortune needed to carry it out!

By contrast, when the American colonists embarked upon their struggle to free themselves from the yoke of bondage imposed on them by George III they were backed by no one but themselves! The Catholic Church in Canada dominated by Jesuits and in whose ranks were to be found several Masons, played a key role in betraying the American cause during the war of 1776 by aiding the traitor Aaron Burr, a one time U.S. Vice President, who reminds me of so many of our past Presidents.

It was the Jesuit Catholics who arranged safe passage for Burr so that he could spy for the British. Another leading figure sent to America by the British-Swiss-Genoa heads of state was Albert Gallatin, a Freemason who inveigled his way into the power structure of the new young country and set about destroying it from the inside. His latter-day counterpart is Paul Volcker, formerly chairman of the Federal Reserve Board during one of the most turbulent periods in U.S. history, and today, in 2009, the economic advisor to President Obama.

William Shelburne, the Master Mason, master spy and

mastermind of the French Revolution, coordinated the activities of all of those engaged in the struggle to stamp out the dangerous new American Republic before it became a role model for the whole world. Among those enemies was Robert Livingston of the Continental Congress Committee. Shelburne arranged for the title of Leading Scottish Rite Mason to pass from his Grand Master, William Walter, who was in the British Army in 1783, to the new Grand Master, Livingston.

Livingston was enthroned as Grand Master of the Grand Lodge of New York, from which position he never ceased to work for the London-Venice-Genoa-Geneva families, who even today control the major wealth of this world. In this infamous circle was to be found Senators Hillhouse, Pickering, Tracy and Plummer, all of whom were Masons and who played a leadership role in trying to persuade their states to secede from the Union. As I said, they were all Freemasons, as was their confidant and co-plotter, British Ambassador to the U.S., Anthony Mary. When Burr, the Master Mason, was uncovered as a traitor because the plot to seize Louisiana for the British went awry, he fled to his Mason friends in England, just as Roberto Calvi fled to his Scottish Rite Mason friends in England. However, unlike Calvi, who was murdered by his so—called "friends," Burr received a hero's welcome from the Earl of Shelburne. Incidentally, it was John Jacob Astor, who paid for Burr's trip. Astor fully agreed with what Shelburne believed in—worship of the satanic Chaldean cult, a cult so powerful that at one period of history it held the entire Persian Empire in its grip. The Chaldean cult is much condemned by the Christian Bible.

The families in Britain, Genoa, Venice and Switzerland are the descendants of those who directed Freemason

Shelburne to crush the young American Republic. Such opium trade-tainted families as Mallet, Pitt, Dundes, Gallatin, and in America, Livingston, Pickering, plus the nest of traitors at Harvard, form the core of the Eastern Establishment liberals and their antecedents who hate America and who fully intend to crush it, as Shelburne taught them to do 250 years ago.

One of the most persistent in this endeavor was the English "economist" and leading Freemason, Thomas Malthus. Just as Marx was created by a European Jesuit-Masonry conspiracy, so also did they create Malthus.

Malthus was a spy in the employ of the British East India Company, the British colonial raw materials, and asset-stripping organization comparable to day's International Monetary Fund. But the false economic premise for which Malthus became known was actually drafted by another Freemason, Count Ortes, of the Ortes Venetian banking family.

The Venetian Black Nobility, enraged by the activities of the American Benjamin Franklin, commissioned and paid for Freemason Ortes to write a rebuttal to Franklin's work. Essentially, Franklin supported the Biblical injunction to be fruitful and multiply. Franklin held the position that economic prosperity would come through an increase in population. The Black Nobility with their "hunt and gather" mentality believed that only enough of the common herd should be saved to serve them.

They believed in genocide, which is where the Club of Rome got its Global 2000 ideas. Ortes's scribbling on behalf of the "noble" families were very anti-American, anti-Franklin and his ideas were taken up, expounded and expanded by other Freemasons such as Prime Minister William Pitt, and later by Malthus, after he received tutoring and instruction from the Scottish Rite Freemason, Lord Shelburne. Malthus then wrote his work, On Population, as a direct contradiction of Franklin's work.

CHAPTER 18

MALTHUS AND BENJAMIN FRANKLIN

Malthus hated the work of Benjamin Franklin, who was despised by the same families to be found in that list of traitors, "America's 60 Families," issued by Freemason Frederick Lundberg.

These families think they are the "be all and the end all" of America. They think they have an inherent right to decide who shall live and who shall die and who shall decide the fate of America.

The descendants of the 60 families struggled mightily to destroy the American Republic and crush every vestige of it underfoot. Their antecedents are doing the same thing today, continuing where their ancestors left off. This cult-ridden abscess must be excised from the body of America if we are to survive and the sooner the better.

Most of the Americans I have spoken with have little idea of how great is the humiliation and shame we suffered through the Malvinas War, a shame we continue to suffer through the degradation of the war in Iraq, and rightly so. We ought to have stood up the British Freemasons and said "no, we will never betray the memory of a great American patriot." Instead, we allowed the Freemasons in America and Britain to stomp all over John Quincy Adams' grave and to hold their ritual of triumph around his tombstone. I mourned the Malvinas betrayal then, and I do so now in 2009, with the betrayal of our honor in the war in Iraq. It is one of the darkest pages to be found in our history. We should not forget it. We should work to remove the oligarch families and controllers of America's destiny out of the Malvinas and to restore it to its rightful owners, the people of Argentina. We should not rest until the memory of the 20,000 sailors of the American fleet, captured and enslaved by British Navy before the War of 1812, is avenged.

As long as we allow the British "noble families" governance of the Malvinas, we can never again revere the name and the memory of a great American, John Quincy Adams. For as long as we fail to do so, we dare call ourselves a God-fearing Christian nation. Three betrayals that rankle the most are Malvinas, South Africa and Zimbabwe. I for one cannot rest while the perpetrators of those crimes remain unpunished; crimes which were planned and enacted by powerful elements of the Freemasonic movement, and carried out by their American servants in the U.S. government.

It is the "60 Families," the ancestors of the Eastern Liberals today, who fought against the American Revolution and republicanism and who planned and caused one tragedy after another in the ensuing years, not the least of which is the cult- ridden, Satan-dominated United Nations. It is these families and their antecedents, which have given us the Masonic-Gnostic- Brahmin Illuminati-Isis, Osiris and Dionysus cults instead of the pure Gospel of Christ.

These are the members of the Liberal Establishment. The

people who gave us the ancient and accepted Scottish Rite (American) Freemasonry underground, established officially only in 1929, but actually founded in 1761, and so very, very active in its war against the young American nation. In passing I would say that the noted historian, Lady Queensborough, says that the rites are based on ancient Kabalistic origins.

Albert Mackey, the man who exposed Masonry, said the following:

> Masonry promises men salvation by ceremonies invented by men, administered by priests, and inhabited by devils. This is the sum and substance of all the false religions on Earth and will ultimately united them against Christ. But the only opponent Masonry dreads is Christ, who refused to worship Satan, and his followers.

The "salvation" promised by Masonry almost led to the successful thwarting of the American Republic in 1812 and in 1861, the terrible War between the States, the so-called "Civil War, " that took over 400,000 lives, which fact has never been emphasized by the Establishment historians (the only kind allowed in the U.S.). This terrible toll exceeds the number of Americans soldiers killed in the First and Second World Wars! Think carefully about this fact, and memorize it because attempts are being made, to sweep these vital statistics under the carpet by our so-called "historians."

And what was the excuse for the War Between the States? Ostensibly, the war was fought to emancipate the negro, but the vast majority of us know now that it was for other reasons.

It is interesting to note that the Northern slave trading families made their fortunes out of the very thing they condemned. They combined slave trading with opium running to China, and that is how the blue blood Oxford and the Harvard graduates and the "noble" families in and around Boston, amassed their "old" money, and in which drug trade their descendants are still involved, today. However, I must leave the stench of slavery and the opium trade and the "Olympians" and the dope drenched "ruling class" and get onto the main subject at hand.

Let me say again in passing, that every one of the families who think of themselves as the elite "royal families" of America made their money out of the opium and slave trade. Tell that to the author of America's Sixty Families and see him run for cover! Mr. Lundberg, of course, would never dream of exposing his famous clients. I want now to move on to later events following the Civil War, which was instigated and run by a Freemason conspiracy from the beginning to the end, through such people as Caleb Cushing and Lloyd Garrison.

There is no doubt that the instigators of the conspiracy to wreck America, which culminated in the War Between the States, were all Scottish Rite Freemasons on both sides of the conflict. It is worth mentioning in passing that the assassination of President Lincoln was also a Jesuit-Freemason plot.

Those Masons allied to the Venetian Black Nobility families, the Contarini and the Pallavicini, and the Jesuit spy network could not have murdered Lincoln without the connivance of the Eastern Establishment families and the Cecil family in England. Thus, Robert Fludd's Rosicrucian Jesuit cult triumphed over the American people, their Constitution and their Republic, and reveled in the murder of the President as one of their "trophies."

What then was the motive behind the Freemason conspiracy to destroy the United States and establish a One World Government? The motive was hatred, deep and fanatical hatred of the republic ideal, the idea that men could be free of serfdom and the feudalistic power exercised by the Old Venetian, Genoese and British families.

The very notion that under a republican form of government, men are free to challenge any decision they do not agree with by exercising their vote, was utterly repugnant to these self-styled rulers. They felt as they still do, that the sole right to decide the fate of the common man rests with them. That is why the Christian religion, with its emphasis on individual freedom, is the target of their hatred and why so many of those old families loved the slave trade and the opium trade as they do the dope trade today. Man was and is nothing to them, of no consequence, merely to be exploited. As Prince Metternich once said: "For me, mankind begins with barons." Incidentally, Metternich was the hero and role model for Henry Kissinger. These old families could act thus because they do not believe in a real and living God! It is true they will from time to time pay lip service to God and Christianity, as we see in the case of the British Royal Family. But they do not believe that God exists!

More than that, this interlocking force of Eastern Establishment families, the Jesuit-Scottish Rite

Rosicrucian banking families of Venice, London, Genoa, Boston, Geneva, Lausanne, Berne, etc. hate with an almost violent obsession, a mercantile society based on industrial growth and technology, resting on industrial capitalism.

The motivating force, the reason for a One World conspiracy such as we see in its visible elements, the Club of Rome, the Mont Pelerin Society, the Cini Foundation, the Bilderbergers, and the Trilateral Commission, the Royal Society for International Affairs, the Council on Foreign Relations and the Aquarians, is the destruction of the Christian religion first, followed by other religions (particularly the Muslim religion) and an end to industrial growth, destruction of technology and a return to feudalism and the New Dark Ages, coupled with a huge reduction in population that their plans require, because the millions of "useless eaters" will no longer be needed in a postindustrial society.

My many "Firsts" include works on the Bellagio interreligious conference, the Global 2000 Report, an expose of the existence of the most secret Freemason lodge, the Quator Coronati Lodge, and the Club of Rome, zero growth and a Post Industrial Society; the plot to launch a Holy War in Jerusalem, starting with an attack on the Dome of the Rock Mosque.

Other exposures include Who Murdered President John F. Kennedy, The P2 Masonic Conspiracy, Who Shot Pope John Paul II, the murder of Roberto Calvi, and Haig's role in the Israeli invasion of Lebanon. Today, the conspiracy by the Freemasons as servants of the Black Nobility and its American "aristocracy" is well advanced. As I predicted 20 years ago, the steel industry, shipbuilding, machine tooling and the footwear industries have all been destroyed; the same thing is happening in Europe.

As for the Global 2000 Report, by refusing food to the starving nations of Africa, millions of black Africans died. Thousands have also died of the HIV-AIDS virus. Limited wars declared desirable and necessary by arch-Satanist, Freemason Bertrand Russell and "Dr. Strangelove" Leo Szilard, and his Shakti Ishtar devil-worshipping cult are in progress in Iran, Central America, South Africa, the Middle East and the Philippines etc.

My answer is that the Christian Bible reads: "God looked down upon them (the pre-Adamites) and saw that they had not prospered." God sent us to help these people to perform their function on Earth, whatever it may be, and I have no idea what it is, but not to murder them. Szilard and his friend, Bertrand Russell, bemoaned the fact that wars had not got rid of enough people as described in Russell's 1923 work, Prospects of Industrial Civilization, from which the following extract is taken:

> Socialism, especially International Socialism, is only possible as a stable system if the population is stationary or nearly so. A slow increase might be coped with by improvements in agricultural methods, but a rapid increase must in the end reduce the whole population.

Russell's false notions are based on the satanic Malthusian principles, which in turn are based on a hatred of nation states, republicanism and a mercantile industrial capitalized state. In 1951 Russell wrote The Impact of Science upon Society, and here are some of the most important ideas that this work espouses:

War has hitherto been disappointing in this respect (i.e. population reduction) but perhaps bacteriological war may prove more effective. If a Black Death (the middle Ages and HIV plague) could spread through the world once in every generation, the survivors could procreate freely, without making the world too full. The State of Affairs might be unpleasant, but what of it? Really high-minded people are indifferent to happiness, especially other people's happiness.

A self-described peacemaker, Russell was a false prophet of Masonry and the leader of the CND, the Campaign for Nuclear Disarmament.

He was the voice of the prophet of the Jesuit-Freemason-Rosicrucian-Black Nobility-American Eastern Establishment. These self-styled rulers of the world become so arrogant that sometimes, they can no longer remain silent. Just note the reference to the Black Plague that swept the world in the middle Ages.

The plague was no "Act of God" since, of course, God is not a murderer, although we often blame Him for the deaths of people, but in my opinion, based on 30 years of research, it was a deliberate act by the antecedents of today's "Olympians" the "Club of 300." This is no far-fetched theory.

True, I have not yet proved it, but there are too many pointers and straws in the wind to ignore it. Just as Dr. Leo Szilard is portrayed in the movie Dr. Strangelove as fiction, so the deadly viruses presently held by the conspirators and portrayed in the movie The Andromeda Strain were also portrayed as fiction in this movie. But it is not fiction. Don't overlook the fact that alchemists and the Black Nobility have carried out medical experiments since the 14th Century.

The deadly viruses against which the miracle drug myosin is totally and utterly ineffective are presently being stored in the CDC under the tightest security. Contrary to the official version, these all the viruses have not been incinerated.

That ought to convince you that my predictions are not mere empty words. We shall see far more "black plagues" in the 21st Century—new and strange plagues we don't know what to call, as well as new and deadlier strains of cholera, malaria and tuberculosis. Let no one say that we were not warned of the pandemics that will encompass the Earth seven fold and carry off millions of people. After all, the goals of the "300" have been clearly spelled out. We need only look at the words of Aurelio Peccei, founder of the Club of Rome who in 1969 said, " … man is a cancer on the world."

CHAPTER 19

IS FREEMASONRY COMPATIBLE WITH CHRISTIANITY?

For centuries Freemasonry has striven to pass the movement off as fully compatible with Christianity. "There is no bar against a Mason being a Christian" is one of Masonry's oldest claims. In this book, I will attempt to draw comparisons between what I call New Testament Christianity and its most daunting enemy, Freemasonry. What evidence I have been able to gather comes mainly from relatives of Masons and ex-Masons, who spoke with me on condition that they not are identified. Those who break the Mason Oath of Secrecy know that the supreme penalty for such transgression is, more often than not, death.

There have literally been thousands of books written for and against Masonry. The Catholic Church has been steadfast and resolute in its opposition to Masonry. Protestant churches have unfortunately not been as united against this dangerous enemy as they should be. I shall be dealing with more recent investigations into Masonry. In 1952, I came across a very interesting article entitled, Darkness Visible, by Walton Hannah.

This book is invaluable to any person seeking to pierce the veil of secrecy which has protected Masonry for so many centuries. The same author, Walton Hannah, later published a paper, Should a Christian be a Freemason? A Mason inside Christianity, the Reverend R.C. Meredith, accepted this challenge to the secrets of Masonry. Very boldly, the Reverend Meredith challenged the church to prove that a Mason could also be a Christian.

Meredith, who studied at Oxford, moved in leftist circles and took part in various pro-left debates, which where very popular in the 1930's. It was the period in British history when it was chic to be a Socialist, when Fabian socialism was off and running, when it was fashionable to work for the Soviet Union, the same period that gave us Bulwer, Lytton, Alfred Milner and Kim Philby. The Milner Group eventually transformed itself into what today is called the Royal Institute for International Affairs (RIIA).

The Reverend Meredith boldly introduced a proposal that an Anglican Church enquiry be launched into Masonry. His proposal to the 1951 Church Assembly read as follows:

> That in view of the widespread publicity which has been given to he article by Walton Hannah, a Commission be appointed, including among its members persons learned in the science of Comparative Religions, to examine the statements made by Mr. Hannah in that article, the attention of the House of Bishops should be directed to anything therein set forth.

It is very interesting to note that Meredith refers to Masonry, however obliquely, as a religion. So confident was Meredith that his resolution would be adopted, and Masonry given a whitewash by the hundreds of Anglican hierarchy Masons who occupy powerful positions inside the Church, that he didn't even bother to place any constraints upon the proposed enquiry. This was highly unusual. When Masons permit the Church to conduct an enquiry into their secret society, it is generally under the most severe restrictions that make the outcome a foregone conclusion; Masonry and the Christian Church are indeed compatible. Since Walton Hannah's work was published in 1952, in the various General Synods of the Anglican Church, there has been a growing concern regarding the true nature of Masonic oaths, the need for secrecy, which is such an integral part of Masonry, the true role of Masonry and the scope of its general and secret activities. Those who seek to blow the lid off Masonry and expose its dark secrets often quote General Ludendorf. More latterly, Masonry has been described as a "type of Mafia" or "the only way to make rapid progress for anyone in commerce or in government."

When real progress was being made in this direction, i.e. when Church enquiries looked like succeeding, the jackals of the press cried "witch hunt." To talk about Masonry in its true colors, to rip the mask from off the benign face of Masonry, became a risky business. Masonry always answered allegations about abuses and excuses laid at its door as "only one example of a bad case among millions of examples of the good that Masonry does."

The sinister mafia aspects of Masonry were never openly discussed which explains why Masonry was so bold about Meredith's resolution; they knew it would pass-muster, and it did. Stephen Knight's book, The Brotherhood; the Secret World of Masonry, published in 1984, immediately ran into that kind of response. Critics, literary and religious leaders branded this excellent work as "badly researched, full of unconfirmed data."

To attempt to describe Masonry is an onerous task. One can say it is the largest fraternal order in the world with unofficially close to 3.5 million members in the U.S. alone. Over 50,000 books and shorter works have been written on the subject since 1717 when Masonry first announced itself.

It has aroused more hatred than any other secular body in the world. Men of the Mormon and Catholic faiths cannot join it. It is outlawed in a few countries. Masonry was declared illegal by Hitler and Mussolini and later, by General Franco. The London Metropolitan hierarchy is substantially Mason.

Among Masons, Kings and potentates are numerous among them: Edward VII, Edward VIII, Frederick the Great, King Haakon of Norway and King Stanislous of Poland are just a few examples tat come to mind.

Presidents of the United States who took the Masonic oath were: James Monroe, Andrew Jackson, James K. Polk, James Buchanan, Andrew Johnson, James A. Garfield, Theodore Roosevelt, William Howard Taft, Warren C. Harding, Franklin D. Roosevelt, Harry S. Truman, Lyndon Johnson, Gerald Ford and Ronald Reagan.

Masons in the music field included the composer of "St. Louis Blues" William Handy, John Philip Sousa, Gilbert and Sullivan, Sibelius and Wolfgang Amadeus Mozart, who was murdered for revealing Mason secrets in "The Magic Flute."

Not one of the Knight's critics pointed out that Masonry never confirms data about its darker side, its malevolently evil deeds, and its effect upon the course of history. Mazzini, at times, appeared to confirm some of the evils and misdeeds of Masonry in international geopolitics, but only in the historical context, data already known; alluding always to the influence of Masonry upon such events, but never confirming its role in a clinically scientific way.

To discredit Knight's claim of undue influence in high places in government and the Metropolitan Police Department and especially into the Criminal Investigate Department (CID), and his contention that in excess of 90% of its detective force are Freemasons, one of the highest officers of the Scottish Rite, Lord Hailsham, was chosen by the Grand Council of England to rebut Knight's totally correct charges. The Lord Chancellor of England, using the power and majesty of his office, wrote a letter to the London Times newspaper, ridiculing and belittling Knight's expose. Hailsham's office of patronage was overstaffed with "favored Masons." Because such an august person as Hailsham had written to the venerable institution the Times, the public accepted that Hailsham's denials on behalf of Masonry were right and that Knight was wrong. Knight's well— founded charges were effectively refuted. By this not-so-subtle means does Masonry protect its own. To say that Knight didn't present confirmed data and could therefore be disregarded, was proof of how powerful and all pervading is Freemasonry. This applies equally to the United States of America, Italy, France and Germany.

Offering the case of Roger Hollis as proof that Knight was inaccurate, Freemasonry cites Hollis, head of MI5 during the Second World War, as being a Mason. Hollis was indeed a Mason, who gave vital military secrets to the Soviet Union. He was the subject of an elaborate attempt by Freemasonry to stifle publication of the work of another good author, Peter Wright, whose book exposed the duplicity of Roger Hollis.

Hollis was a man who delivered American and British Military Secrets to the Soviets, and he was a Freemason for most of his adult life. I am only able to refer briefly to this man and his betrayal of U.S. and British to the Soviet Union.

As Wright could not be discredited through letters to the Times, an attempt was made by the "James Bond" SIS team to silence him—permanently. Wright fled to Australia where people in high places protected him. Wright did all he could to get his expose of Roger Hollis published in Australia, but the long arm of Scottish Rite Masonry reached out from Britain and by the most dubious and convoluted reasoning, the Attorney General of Britain went to Australia to argue in Australian courts against the book being published there. Though Freemasonry will deny it and quote lack of documentary evidence to support its denials, my most reliable source in British Intelligence told me that Masonry in Britain and Australia teamed up in a joint effort to stop Wright. The book was scheduled to be printed in Canada, and in a few months later, in Australia On this occasion, Freemasons were not successful in preventing the truth from coming out.

Meanwhile in London, three newspapers defied British censorship and began publishing extracts from Wrights book. Press censorship in Britain is carried out most effectively through the use of what is called "D Notices." If the Home Secretary deems any book, story or article harmful to the state or not in the interest of the country, then publishers, magazine editors, newspapers and so on, receive a "D Notice" restraining them from publishing that particular story named in the "D Notice." If the "D Notice" is disregarded, the Attorney General has the right to prosecute offenders and the courts will generally impose severe sentences on the offender or offenders.

Such is the right of "free speech" and "freedom of the press" protected in Britain. Three London newspapers were placed under indictment for disobeying the "D Notice" they received prohibiting them from publishing Wright's work. The Attorney General described their conduct in exercising their right to "freedom of the press" as a deliberate and gross flouting of the Law. All those who were involved in opposing Wright were Freemasons of the highest degree who strove mightily to protect a deceased 33rd Degree Mason from total exposure. "Poorly researched, lacking in confirmed data?" Possibly, but present events, which later become history, can seldom, if ever, be "confirmed."

We all know the truth about the assassination of John F. Kennedy, and his brother Edward's conduct at Chappaquiddick. But "confirmed data?" It is locked up in legal files and court records for the next 99 years! That is how the Establishment works! The Masons are no different. They protect their own!

Take the case of Commissioner of the City of London Police, James Page. Masons claim his rapid promotions could not have been due to Mason patronage, because, they say, he only joined the secret brotherhood after he became Commissioner. Naturally Lodge secrets remain Lodge secrets. Who can say Page joined the Masons while still a fledgling police officer? Only "discredited" ex-Masons, who are of course written off as liars or worse! Page it seems, if precedent is anything to go by, must have been a Lodge member, long before he became Commissioner of Police.

Then there is the case of permanent officers of government in the financial heart of the world, the City of London. Knight and others, including myself, are well aware of the fact that its most influential members are leadings Freemasons. Yet when Knight actually dared to name these men, it was officially denied, not that they weren't Masons, but that they had not attended meetings of the Guildhall Lodge on the dates mentioned by Knight.

Because of their high rank, the Masons were believed rather than Knight, who was subsequently accused of "gross inaccuracies." I have digressed into the subject of providing "documentary proof and "confirmed data" in the face of Masons in positions of great power and influence, who close ranks when attacked. "Factual inaccuracies" is how the Guildhall Lodge members disposed of Mr. Knight's expose of how the Mason Brotherhood controls the City of London—and Westminster for that matter.

Knight provides a convincing explanation of how Mason registers of English Lodges worldwide are "sealed" against investigators. In the case of Roger Hollis, the Far East registers of Masons were clamped shut against both Knight and Wright and it was sufficient for Masonry to deny that Hollis was ever a Mason for both authors to be discredited for "lack of confirmed data." After all, the public tends to believe Edward the Duke of Kent rather than relatively unknown authors. If Masonry could depose

Edward VII and blame his fall on Mrs. Wallis Simpson, then, to brand two excellent authors' works as "factually inaccurate and lacking in confirmed data," was a relatively easy task.

Another very good expose of Freemasonry is the paper written and published by Walton Hannah called, Darkness Visible, which came under the most severe attack not only by leading Mason members under the hierarchy of the Anglican Church, but by so-called literary critics and self-appointed "experts," there to defend Masonry. Any enquiry into the provenance of initiation texts and rituals used by Freemasonry, would on its own be a work of a life time and would probably, even then, be dubbed as "lacking in confirmed data" by a united and aroused Brotherhood of Masonry.

My in-depth study of Masonry over the past thirty years has taught me a great deal about the "Brotherhood," more particularly that to fully document even the initiation oaths, texts and rituals of initiation, would take the combined efforts of several genuinely accredited experts on comparative religions. Thus, by the very nature of such a vast undertaking, Masonry has always been able to continue to draw a cloak of secrecy about itself, which is hard to penetrate.

To make a case against the sinister brotherhood is exceedingly difficult. Many have tried with varying degrees of success, but in general, it is true to say that notwithstanding the scores of outstanding books, which have exposed Masonry for what it is, Masonry emerged relatively unscathed.

If an opinion poll,-not those politically motivated, professionally manufactured opinion polls which elect politicians to office—were to be taken, I have reason to believe that 70% of the general public would say that Freemasonry is a benevolent society doing a lot of good for the community!

In an Anglican Church Assembly debate in 1951, it became clear that the "benevolent" and "charitable" work carried out by Freemasonry remained upper-most in people's impressions of Masonry. There are a number of works, which point out that "charitable work" such as street collections in aid of various charities, are really not charitable at all, since it is the public and not Freemasonry that donates the money. Were Mason Lodges to publically and consistently contribute large sums of money to charitable institutions, its benevolent face might not be the mask that it truly is. It is true to say that most informed members of the public never ask the question "why do we allow such an ultra-secret society to operate in our midst and, what goes on behind its closed doors?"

It cannot be otherwise, for how can the lady whose husband goes off to Lodge meetings know anything about Masonry's strict secrecy laws, its Craft Degrees and the Holy Royal Arch, let alone its "omerta" sealed lips policy. Should she be of an enquiring mind and ask probing questions, her husband would tell her only about the sumptuous banquets and fund-raising activities for charity, but more than this, she would not learn anything. No wonder the public's perception is far removed from the truth of what Freemasonry really is!

CHAPTER 20

WHEN, WHERE AND HOW DID FREEMASONRY ORIGINATE

L iterature on Freemasonry fills the shelves of most public libraries, except that works by authors who came uncomfortably close to the truth are not available. If one enquires from the librarian, answers vary from "we have never had it" or else "it was withdrawn some time ago."

There are many books available which purport to prove that there is no connection between "modern" Masonry, King Solomon and the Druids. These "expert technical books on Masonry" as one librarian described them to me, always pour cold water on the connection between Masonry and the ancient Egyptian Isis cult, Dionysus and so forth.

Even Walton Hannah displays reluctance as a scientist to fully commit himself. In his work, Christians by Degrees, Hannah states:

> If as they do, modern Masons claim to be stewards and guardians of ancient mysteries of which they are the legitimate heirs, all that can be conceded to them is that there are indeed striking parallels and resemblances, even in the actual signs and symbols; symbolism is however very— hard to be precise and dogmatic

about, it is hardly remarkable that Freemasonry and Masonic mysteries today show great similarities to ancient mysteries and religions which have many points in common with Masonic mysteries.

Libraries are filled with books which seek to deny the connection between Masons and Rosicrucians while the serious student of Masonry knows that the connection is very strong. Sir Roger Besomt was an upper-degree Mason in the Egyptian Rite and it is a well-established fact that he was certainly deeply involved in both Theosophy and Rosicrucian. Let's take the British Royal family for example. Many of its members, including Prince Charles and the Duke of Kent are involved with Rosicrucian No one denies that both are Masons. Masonry has never given a proper answer to the three W's where, why when and where did Freemasonry originate? Masons have always categorically denied that it was formed to be a counter to Christianity and that it is not a religion, but their denials wear thin as we shall presently begin to see.

John Hamill, a master apologist for Masonry and its Librarian and Curator of the Grand Lodge Library and Museum, states:

> Modern Lodges are very much like those which existed in the 17th Century.

His idea of Mason history is as follows:

> The Grand Lodge of England was formed on 24th June 1717, and a rival Ancients Grand Lodge was formally constituted in 1751; and that these two rival Grand Lodges joined together on 27th December 1713, to

form the United Grand Lodge of England, much as we know it today.

But Hamill doesn't tell us, why the need for a secret society at all?

- ❖ What is Freemasonry?
- ❖ Why do men seek to join it?
- ❖ What is the true nature of the organization whose obligations they must accept if they do join?

In spite of the thousands of books, which tell us what Freemasonry is, there are still many things about it that we do not fully know. In early 1850's, the Grand Lodge of England published a pamphlet, What every candidate should know, which says inter alia:

> Freemasonry is a society of men historically linked together with medieval operative Masons, from whom they derive their private means of recognition, their ceremonial, and many of their customs. Its members adhere to ancient principles of Brotherly love (a Marxist idea—JC) relief and truth not only among themselves but also in their relations with the world at large and by ritual percepts and example.

Now if that explains anything in a truly meaningful manner, then I confess that it's true meaning escape me. Librarian Hamill however, tries to give a more detailed "explanation" by saying:

> The candidate for initiation learns very early in his Masonic career that the basic principles of Freemasonry are brotherly love, relief and truth.

He then goes on to attempt to equate Marxism with brotherly love by stating:

> Brotherly love in its sense of the promotion of tolerance and respect for the beliefs and ideals of others, and the building of a world in that respects tolerance together with kindness and tolerance and understanding. Relief is not in the sense of monetary giving only nor limited to it, but giving in the widest sense of the word, charitable giving of money, (but never their own—JC) time and effort to assist the community as a whole. Truth in the sense of striving for high moral standards, and in conducting one's life—in all its aspects—in an honest a manner as possible. In simple terms, a Freemason is taught his duties to his God (which God is not stated—JC) and the laws of his country.

Such a preposterous explanation of what Masonry is, unfortunately is what most of the general public believes. When one points to the most notable exceptions to this would-be noble body of men, such as the morals of some of its highest, adherents, its charitable monetary contributions that emanate not from Masonry but from public donations, its disregard for the law of the country i.e. the French and Bolshevik Revolutions, one is met with outright denials or as in the case of Roberto Calvi, that it is "a notable exception" such as might occur once in a century! Every Freemason spokesman denies that the secret society is a religion. In 1985, the Board of the General Purposes of the United Grand Lodge published a pamphlet entitled, Freemasonry and Religion.

Among other denials, the Board states as follows:

Freemasonry is not a religion, nor is it a substitute for religion. Freemasonry lacks the basic elements of a religion, but is far from indifferent to religion.

Without interfering in religious practice it expects each member to follow his own faith and to place above all other duties the duty to his God, by whatever name He is known. Freemasonry is thus a supporter of religion.

A Working Group of the Grand Lodge stated further:

Freemasonry knows that its rituals do not amount to the practice of religion.

A more bold and barefaced lie is difficult to imagine. Not only is Masonry a religion, it is very definitely an anti-Christian religion aimed at the destruction of Christianity.

❖ How can Masonry justify its claim to be a non-religion when its rituals are centered and based upon altars, temples and chaplains?
❖ Why are prayers recited, such as the prayer explicitly stated as such in Mason literature, in the Emulation Ritual for the First Degree?

Let us examine this "non-religion" prayer:

Vouchsafe Thine aid. Almighty Father and Supreme Governor of the Universe, to our present convention and grant that this candidate for Freemasonry may so dedicate and devote his life to Thy service as to become a true and faithful brother among us. Endue him with a competency of Thy divine wisdom, that, assisted by the secrets (emphasis added) of our Masonic art, he may the better be enabled to unfold the beauties of true goodliness to the honor and glory of Thy Holy Name.

If that isn't religion, then nothing in this world is! The question that needs to be answered is "what kind of a religion is Masonry?"

In the Second Degree, there is an actual prayer, which goes like this:

We supplicate the continuance of Thine aid, O merciful Lord, on behalf of ourselves and him who kneels before Thee. May the work begun in Thy Name be continued to Thy Glory and evermore established in us by obedience to Thy percepts.

The fact that the God Masons prays to is Satan is carefully hidden from all Masons except those who reach the exalted 33rd Degree! The name of Jesus is always very specifically excluded. As Christ our Lord says in His Gospels:

He who is not for Me, is against Me.

There is another prayer in the Third Degree which invokes the blessing of God and of Heaven upon the new member:

Almighty and Eternal God, Architect and Ruler of the Universe, at whose creative fiat all things were first made.

Masonry is most careful in that while it makes liberal use of Christian prayers, which are easily recognized as such, it scrupulously avoids all Christian references. By this singular action of excluding the name of Christ from its "prayers" Masonry denies the very existence and authority of Jesus. If as Masons aver it is not a religion well and good; but, why copy Christian prayers and then delete absolutely the name of Christ? Does not such conduct indicate that Masonry is anti-Christ?

I firmly believe that Masonry stands for anti- Christ behavior, and moreover, this is the answer to the "why" masonry was established in the first place! In support of my claim that Masonry is an anti-Christ religion, I offer the Opening Ceremony of the Royal Arch prayer which goes like this:

> Omnipotent God unto whom all hearts are open, all desires known, and from whom no secrets are hid, cleanse the thoughts of our hearts by the inspiration of Thy Holy Spirit, that we may perfectly love Thee and magnify Thee.

Any member of the Anglican Church will instantly recognize this wholly Christian prayer. The significance of this particular "Masonic prayer" is that the all-important words "through Jesus Christ our Lord" is excised.

Christ said that those who deny Him are of the anti-Christ. By excising the name of Christ from this prayer Masons demonstrate their disregard of Christ. They are therefore to be counted in the ranks of the anti-Christ forces of Satan.

The Closing Ceremony of the Royal Arch also makes use of a well-known Christian prayer, namely, "Glory be to God on High on Earth, peace and Goodwill towards men," but fails to mention that these words are taken from the Gospel of Our Lord Jesus Christ. In my mind and in the minds of many serious students of Freemasonry, the foregoing examples of religious activities voids Masonry's claim that it is not a religion, and proves to the world, that it indeed is a religion.

The Grand Lodge responded to a challenge from me by saying:

> … As Freemasonry is not a religion or a substitute for it, there is no reason why the name of Christ should be mentioned in its rituals.

The answer to this denial is surely to pose another question: "If what you say is correct, that Masonry is not a religion, why then have you taken prayers from the Christian Bible, why do you constantly refer to temples and alters, and why do you, while using phrases from the Christian Bible deny the very existence of Jesus Christ by cutting out His name from every one of the prayers you have copied from Him?" There is never a doubt that Mason "prayers" are frequently based on Christian liturgies. Why then does Masonry deny that it is a religion, and why does Masonry assiduously delete the name of Christ from its Christian-copied prayers?

Prayers are an integral part of Mason rituals, so how can Masonry deny that it is a religion? Masons say that their prayers contain no element of worship. Yet, the ceremony leader is called a "Worshipful Master" and I leave it to you to decide whether the prayers, Mason prayers I have given you are not acts of worship? No one, with the exception of perhaps Alice in Wonderland can believe that Mason prayers are distinguishable from "worship." Which raises another vital point?

Even if Mason insistence upon such distinctions of "prayer" and "worship" and "non-religion" could be accepted, and clearly it cannot be so, the deliberate omission of the name of Christ and the Gospels of Jesus Christ from whence their "prayers" came, plus the omission of the Christian basic cornerstone belief that none come to God save and except through our Lord Jesus Christ, is a slight and an affront to the Christian religion.

It denies the Divinity of Christ. No doubt about it. How then can men who claim to be Christians also be Masons? Christ said one "cannot serve two masters." By accepting Mason ritual, Masons in effect also deny His existence. It follows that one cannot be for Him, while at the same time being against Him!

There is absolutely no way that Freemasonry can deny that it is "neither a religion nor a substitute for religion." The evidence to the contrary is overwhelming! Nor can Mason defenders bring evidence to show that by excluding the name of Christ they are not rejecting Him, because it is not merely a case of deliberate exclusion, it is a case of deliberate insult by omission. Masonic apologists tell us "our prayers are not acts of worship but merely a request for blessing at the opening of our rituals and a returning of thanks at the close for blessings received." How does this differ from religious worship?

The obvious fact is that it does not! Mason rituals everlastingly invoke the name of God, often in distinctive terms, such as Great Architect of the Universe (as in the

First Degree); Grand Geometrician (Second Degree); the Most High, the Almighty and the Eternal God (Third Degree); the Supreme Being. GAOL) (Great Architect of the Universe). Who are these Gods?

Does Masonry worship a Supreme Being, or as it sometimes says, only a belief in a Supreme Being? There would be no Mason rituals without involving a Divine name. The Freemason pamphlet I referred to earlier, Free-masonry of Religion published by the Masonic Board for General Purposes, glosses over the Masonic God by stating:

> Freemasons meet in common respect for the Supreme Being as He remains Supreme for their individual religions and it is no part of Freemasonry to join religions together.

Since the Western World is Christian whether some like it or not. Masonry must have great problems with a neutral inter-faith service. We, as Christians, cannot escape the very essence of our religion, namely that Christ is preeminent as the Son of God. Masonry says it does not wish to "offend" other religions. How does it do this if it excludes the name of Christ? Is it excluded so that it does not offend the B'nai Brith (Sons of the Covenant) Jewish Freemasonry? Masonry has sought for hundreds of years to avoid "giving offence" to other religions, but does not hesitate to offend Christians by excising the name of Christ from its ritual prayers.

"Inter-faith" services can only be successful where Christianity takes second place. It follows therefore that Christians cannot be Masons; either they must approve of

Christianity downgraded or else resign from Masonry. Before Masons reach the exalted heights of the higher Degrees, many believe that while praying they are praying to the God of their religion. But once they reach the "closed shop" of the Mason Hierarchy, there is no doubt but that their prayers are expressly directed to Satan.

Christianity has no secrets! Any person who can read can read the glad Gospel. Why do Masons find overwhelming secrecy such a necessity? The Masonic creed and its attendant rituals are filled with "secret words."

Why should this be the case, unless deception is intended? We hear so many times "compound words," "I am and I shall be."

Freemasonry says it is not obliged to support Christianity. Why then does Masonry borrow so much of the trappings of Christianity, if it doesn't support it? The ceremonies of the Holy Arch, perhaps more than any other ceremony, employ "sacred words." The center-piece of the Holy Arch Ceremonies is the pedestal—the Alter on top of which appear the "sacred words." It is clear that despite its protestations to the contrary.

Freemasonry is a religion when the explanation of the Sacred Words takes place. Here it is beyond dispute that Masonry is a religion in opposition to Christianity.

Let us examine the Ritual of the Royal Arch, which is the climax of what is called "Craft Masonry:"

It is intimately blended with all that is nearest and dearest to us in a future state of existence; divine and human affairs are interwoven so awfully and minutely in all its disquisitions. It has virtue for its aim; the Glory of God for its object, and the eternal welfare of man is considered in every part, every point and letter of its ineffable mysteries. Suffice to say, that it is founded on the Sacred Name, J h, who was from the

beginning, is now and will remain one and the same forever, the Being necessarily existing in and from Himself in all actual perfection, original in His essence.

This Supreme Degree inspires its members with the most exalted ideas of God, leads to the purest and most devout piety, a reverence for the incomprehensible J h, the eternal Ruler of the Universe, the elemental and primordial source of all its principles, the very spring and fount of all its virtues.

The "mystery" word "J h" is Jabulon, a "sacred" name. It is a composite word interchangeable with Jehovah.

One may certainly by now be left in no doubt that Freemasonry is a religion whose primary function is to be a secret counterforce to the Christian religion, a revolutionary order, capable of controlling political events.

CHAPTER 21

FREEMASONRY AND MEMBERS OF THE BRITISH ROYAL FAMILY

Added to the above, we discover that Masonry actually has so— called Christian Degrees such as the Red Cross of Constantine, the Rose Croix, which is very important in Mason Legends.

To qualify for the Rose Croix (of which the British Royal family are members), calls for prior membership of the Seventeen Degrees of the Ancient Accepted Rite of Freemasonry. The Duke of Connaught and Duke of Kent are believed to be members of both Orders. The Grand Master of the Grand Lodge of England, the Duke of Connaught was a master for twenty years. Other royal family members of this Lodge include Edward VII.

According to a letter written by the Grand Secretary on August 5, 1920, George I, and George III, who was King at the time of the American Revolution, both belonged to the Grand Lodge of England. According to the abovementioned letter:

> … Everyone who comes into Freemasonry is enjoined at the outset not to countenance any act which may have a tendency to subvert the peace and good order of society.

One marvels at this when it is realized that Grand Lodge member, the Earl of Shelburne, trained Danton and Marat, before turning them loose on France to wreak the havoc of the French Revolution. Being a member of the Grand Lodge didn't save King Edward VII, when his fellow-Masons decided to get rid of him rather than run the risk of not going to war with Germany in 1939. Now, again, we note the strong allusion to religion. "Every English Lodge at its consecration is dedicated to God and His service; no one can become a Mason until he has declared his faith in the Supreme Being," the General Secretary wrote in 1905. Masonry took the offensive again in 1938 because of increasing disquiet about its activities. Here again, belief in the Supreme Being was paramount.

The General Secretary said in his 1938 statement:

> The Bible is always open in the Lodges. It is called, The Volume of the Sacred Law. Every candidate is required to take his Obligation on that book, or on the Volume which is held by his particular creed to impart sanctity to an oath or promise taken upon it.

This implies that the Bible is probably not the only "sacred volume" on display. The Bible is for purely decorative purposes and is there for members in the lower degrees (from the First to the Fourth Degrees). As all serious students of Masonry will know, secret societies became all the fashion in the 17th Century, in much the same way, as it was chic to be a Socialist in the late 1920's-early 1930's. Right up to April 1747, Masons still paraded through city streets, but following an order from the Grand Master, thereafter they went underground. As far back as 1698, a pamphlet was circulated called, To All Godly People in City of London, it exhorted readers:

... to take care lest their ceremonies and secret swearing take hold of you; and be wary that none cause you to err from Godliness; for this devilish Sect of Men Meet in Secret. For how should men meet in secret places and with secret sign taking care that none observe them to do the Work of God.

What "secrets" did the pamphlet refer to? It is the same then as it is now, signs, grips, and words used to prove membership. These secret signs are said to have emanated from medieval stone masons, who swore never to pass their skills on to "outsiders," and were recognized as fellow-craftsmen by certain handshakes-grips, etc. Nothing has changed. Although it is unlikely that any stonemasons are in Freemasonry today, their "grips" and handshakes remain the premier recognition sign. But Masonry today is more than that; it is a very sinister secret society in which members are sworn to secrecy by deadly Oaths of the most chilling kind.

Clearly no Christian Society would enforce a code of silence by threatening its members with horrible death if the code were breached. Masonry may deceive the members in the Lower Degrees to believe it is based on Christianity, but in 1723, Dr. James Anderson, a Presbyterian Minister-Mason said:

> This now thought more expedient to oblige them (members of the Brotherhood) to that Religion which all men agree, leaving their particular opinions to themselves.

In 1813 the Grand Lodge stated its position as follows:

> Let a man's religion or mode of worship be what it may, he is not excluded from the order, provided he believes in the glorious architect of Heaven and Earth and practice the sacred duty of morality.

Thus was established a comprehensive outlook toward religions, which is totally at war with Christianity.

This concept is anti-Christian because it presumes that all religions can be encapsulated in an all-embracing concept of the Great Architect. Christ specifically condemned this approach.

Therefore it is safe to conclude that Freemasonry is not compatible with Christianity and that it is indeed a religion at variance with Christianity.

By 1816, whatever might have existed of the Christian religion in Freemasonry was removed, so that the Universal God concept could be fostered enabling men of all religions to take part in Lodge rituals. Dr. James Anderson carried out the "restructuring" of Freemason rituals in England, the Presbyterian minister I have just talked about:

> Belief in the G (reat) A (rchitect) O(f) T (he) U (niverse) and his revealed will, shall be an essential qualification for membership.

Freemasonry claims that it never invites or solicits men to join. In the booklet, Information for the Guidance of Members, which every new Mason receives, it states (on page 22):

The question of improper solicitation of candidates has been raised on many occasions and the Board feels that a statement on this matter would be helpful. There is no objection (emphasis added) to a neutrally worded approach being made to a man who is considered a suitable candidate for Freemasonry. There can be no objection to his being reminded, once, that the approach has been made (emphasis added). So not only do Masons solicit new members, but once approached, they are "reminded." The booklet goes on to say:

The potential candidate should then be left to make his own decision without further solicitation.

This piece of advice on soliciting new members was originally adopted by the Board of General Purposes, December 9, 1981. Thus, when a candidate at his initiation signs that he joined of his own free will, it may not in every case be the truth. Once initiated, it is possible for a diligent Mason to "raise" himself from Apprentice to the Third Degree of "Master Mason."

Such men are carefully watched as possible candidates for higher secrets, where the real truth about Masonry lies. But the vast majority of Freemasons never get "raised" above the Third Degree or Fourth Degrees. The first three degrees definitely account for the bulk of Mason membership. The so-called Higher Degrees are also known as "Further Degrees," from Secret Master to Grand Inspector General, and in England are controlled by their own Supreme Council resident in Duke Street, St James London. (This is one of many "Grace and Favor" houses belonging to the Queen of England.)

Initiation into these Degrees is open to Master Masons selected by the Supreme Council. These Master Masons are usually "talent-spotted" early by the Secret Master who attends various Lodge meetings "incognito" for that purpose. Only an insignificant number of Freemasons who take the step beyond the Third Degree ever get as far as the mid-point 18th Degree, Knight of the Pelican and Eagle, and Sovereign Prince Rose Croix of Heredom. The further these few go, the greater becomes the number of "dropouts."

The 31st Degree (Grand Inspector Inquisitor Commander) is limited to 400 members. At this level, the true character of Freemasonry is two-thirds exposed. The 32nd Degree of Sublime Prince of the Royal Secret has only 180 members and the 33rd pre-eminent Grand Inspectors General, is restricted to 75 members. These figures of course apply only to Great Britain. By the time a Freemason reaches the 33rd Degree, he is ready to perform any duty he may be ordered to perform.

Wars and revolutions are only a part of the game. "War on God" and "War on Christianity" are two of the favorite cries of 33rd Degree Freemasons when they meet in secret. The 4th to the 14th Degrees are conferred at once and in name only during a special ritual held for this purpose.

The 18th Degree, the 19th and 29th are given during the initiation site of the 30th De gree. This is to force selected candidates to continue to "progress." The 30th Degree is the Grand Elected Knight Kadosh or the Knight of the Black and White Eagle.

The three Degrees starting at the 31st Degree are conferred

FREEMASONRY FROM A TO Z

singly. Masonry has to be sure that a candidate is ready to pass to a scale hitherto unknown to him!

CHAPTER 22

INNOCUOUS MASONRY

N o Mason can go above the 18th Degree without the unanimous agreement of the Supreme Council. The first to third Degrees may be called "innocuous Masonry" because the excesses, both physical and spiritual, the plotting against governments, the hatred of Christ and Christianity are never revealed to any Mason below the 25th Degree. It is no small wonder that 3rd Degree Masons and the public in general regard this highly secretive organ in our society as merely a philanthropic society dedicated to the good of all mankind.

The bulk of Mason membership does not trouble itself overly to find out what goes on in the so-called "Higher Degrees " of the Ancient and Accepted Rite. If and when they do or are able to do so, they might well recoil in horror, especially Christians, and give up their Freemasonry membership. Two examples of men, who found out the truth about Masonry and left it, and their anxious reactions to what they had been involved in, are to be found in letters they wrote to their respective churches after exiling Masonry. Naturally their identities cannot be disclosed for fear of reprisals:

> For a long time as a Christian I always strongly defended Masonry, feeling that I would reconcile its philosophies and precepts, supposedly based on

teaching morality and charity—with Christianity. But after being raised to the very higher Degrees, I saw how blind I had been, and how effectively the enemy uses his weapons of subtlety and rationality in the blinding process. It was in the Higher Degrees that I discovered the true evils and horrors of Masonry.

God's spirit opened my spiritual eyes, and allowed me to behold what I was doing. I was in bondage to evil and had not realized it. It was the hardest thing ever not to be "deeply disturbed by obscene sexual images" in his sleep and during his times of prayer. His sub-conscious was deeply imbued with feelings about blood lust, blood and killing of my family and relatives.

The man was a stable, mature, well-adjusted person, with no history of mental disturbances or sexual aberrations of any kind (supported by expert medical opinion). Feeling threatened, he received counseling during which it became evident the sexual imagery, the blood and the knives were linked closely to Freemasonry symbols, the blood and the knife with which he was tempted to kill family members being linked with the Oaths in Free-masonry. After intensive treatment and the laying on of hands by trained priests of the Anglican Church and exhortations by them in the name of Jesus, the disturbing images vanished as soon as he left Freemasonry, and he has never had a recurrence of the images and feelings.

The Oaths in Freemasonry are very carefully hidden from "outsiders." In recent years Masonry has taken even greater care to keep its deadly penalties for breaking Oaths well hidden. In the First degree the following applies: Obligation. Physical penalty omitted. In other words, there are no written penalties these days for physical penalties. They are now entrusted for carrying out to the Higher Degrees from (the 18th Degree). But I have discovered at least part of the written threat for "physical punishment" that goes like this:

> Brother, by your meek and candid behavior this evening you have, symbolically, escaped two great dangers, but there was a third, which traditionally would have awaited you until the last period of your existence. The dangers you have escaped are those of S and S there was likewise this ct with a running N about your N which would have rendered any attempt at retreat fatal.

There is little doubt that the words "with a running N" mean noose around his neck, meaning death by hanging, as Roberto Calvi discovered all too late. The penalties are always thus described. In another printed paper, I found the following:

> To the symbolic penalty at one time included in the obligation (now well-hidden) in this Degree, had he improperly disclosed the secrets entrusted to him, which implied that as a man of honor, a FCFM would rather have had the Iblo, the thtt and the gttrbs of ta or d bts or tap.

(No one other than the 33rd Mason knows the meaning of these symbols.) One can only imagine what punishments are described in these letters. One of the most frightening penalties for breaking Masonic Oaths I came across was the following:

All these points I solemnly swear to observe, without evasion, equivocation or mental reservation of any kind, under no less a penalty, on violation of any of the, that being severed in two, you bowels burned to ashes, and those ashes scattered over the face of the Earth, and wafted by the four cardinal winds of heaven, that no trace or remembrance of so vile a wretch may longer be found among men, particularly Master Masons.

When a Worshipful Master is raised and installed, he receives a warning about the penalty that will certainly follow if he breaks any Oaths and Vows:

To have the right hand struck off and slung over the left shoulder there to wither and decay.

At the initiation ceremony of Exaltation to the Royal Arch of Masonry, the initiate is clearly warned that the penalty attached to the Obligation is "that of suffering the loss of life by having my head-struck off." Nowadays, such direct statements do not appear. Instead the punishments are related in symbols and letters. This has come about only since 1979 when the Grand Master stated that it was no longer "suitable" to express the penalties in their present form. The important thing to remember is that the penalties have not changed! What has changed is that they are now concealed from outsiders!

Thousands of books, both pro and con have been written attempting to answer the question. As a serious student of Freemasonry with thirty years of in-depth research to my credit, my answer is that Freemasonry may be described in the following terms:

- ❖ It is most definitely a closed secret society, which, for reasons unknown is permitted to function in a free and open society such as a Western Christian Democracy.
- ❖ Freemasonry is very definitely a religion based on cults and satanic worship. It is anti-Christ and anti-Christian and long ago dedicated itself to eradicating the Christian faith, although this aim is carefully concealed from the bulk of its membership, especially those in the first three Degrees.
- ❖ It is revolutionary in character and objectives. It is well known that Freemasonry was responsible at least for the planning stages of the French Revolution.
- ❖ Freemasonry stands for the overthrow of the existing order of things, and all religions save one.

Freemasonry demands absolute obedience to its Oaths.

The penalties for failing to observe the secrecy Oath or "betraying" Mason secrets are severe and include death by hanging in extreme cases. Other lesser physical punishment is frequently meted out to those whose break the Oaths.

- ❖ Freemasonry, while pretending to obey the laws of the country, works silently to change laws it deems undesirable.
- ❖ Freemasons are to be found in the highest seats of power in governments of all countries, as well as in the private sector, business and commerce. As such, Freemasonry is an uncontrolled force wielding immense power that can, and has changed the course of history.

❖ Freemasonry is a moral, ethical and philanthropic society only up to the 3rd Degree. The vast majority of Freemasons never progress beyond the 3rd Degree and are therefore unaware of the true nature, aims and objectives of Freemasonry.

❖ Freemasonry is a government operating within an elected government to the detriment of the latter.

❖ The charitable aspect of Freemasonry is a mask and has no credibility, bordering as it does on deception. It is a mask and a cover for Masonry's true objectives.

❖ Freemasonry has done an immense amount of harm to the cause of Christianity and is responsible for the loss of millions of lives in wars and revolutions ever since the French Revolution burst upon France.

❖ The final test is whether it is compatible with Christianity?

❖ Can Christians also be Masons?

To both questions, the answer is a resounding no! I have had claims that Washington DC has many Mason structures built as public or government buildings, and that its layout is in the form of a pentagram. It is difficult to prove or disprove some of the claims, but one building that appears to fit the Mason claim is the Pentagon. The pentagon is an occult symbol. The building was designed by John Whiteside Parsons, a professed Satanist. The architect was George Bergstrom, but it is not known if he had any connection to Masonry.

The true secrets of Masonry may never be revealed to

JOHN COLEMAN

mankind and thus it is very difficult for a writer to escape criticism while examining a subject as complex as Masonry. But that does not mean that no attempt should be made.

If any of the claims I have made are wrong, then I am indeed apologetic, for they are not written in a spirit of blind meanness, and it is hoped that Masons who are better qualified than I am will point these out, so that they may be corrected.

160 |

Other titles

OMNIA VERITAS LTD PRESENTS:

BEYOND the CONSPIRACY
UNMASKING THE INVISIBLE WORLD GOVERNMENT

by John Coleman

All great historical events are planned in secret by men who surround themselves with total discretion.

Highly organized groups always have the advantage over citizens

OMNIA VERITAS LTD PRESENTS:

THE CLUB OF ROME
THE THINK TANK OF THE NEW WORLD ORDER

BY JOHN COLEMAN

The many tragic and explosive events of the 20th century didn't happen by themselves, but were planned according to a well-established pattern...

Who were the planners and creators of these major events?

OMNIA VERITAS LTD PRESENTS:

DIPLOMACY BY DECEPTION
AN ACCOUNT OF THE TREASONOUS CONDUCT BY THE GOVERNMENTS OF BRITAIN AND THE UNITED STATES

BY JOHN COLEMAN

The story of the creation of the United Nations is a classic case of diplomacy by deception

DRUG WAR against AMERICA

BY JOHN COLEMAN

The drug trade cannot be eradicated because its directors will not allow the world's most lucrative market to be taken away from them...

The real promoters of this cursed trade are the "elites" of this world.

ABORTION
GENOCIDE IN AMERICA

BY JOHN COLEMAN

I MAINTAIN THAT WHEN A WOMAN AGREES TO AN ABORTION IN A NON-LIFE THREATENING SITUATION, SHE HAS TAKEN LEAVE OF HER SENSES AND SHOULD BE ADJUDGED "TEMPORARILY INSANE."

ABORTION SHOULD BE EXPLAINED AS EUPHEMISM FOR "MURDER BY DECEPTION"

THE ROTHSCHILD DYNASTY

by John Coleman

Historical events are often caused by a "hidden hand"...

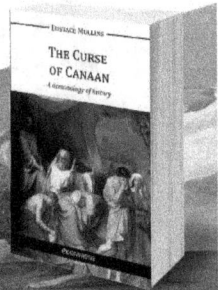
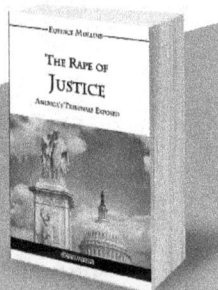

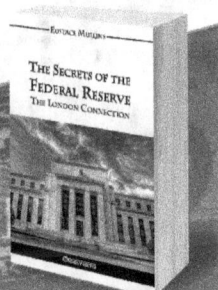

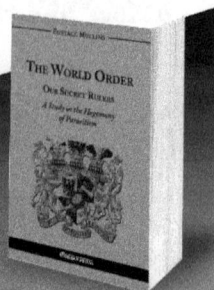

Omnia Veritas Ltd presents:

THE WORLD ORDER

OUR SECRET RULERS

A Study in the Hegemony of Parasitism

by

EUSTACE MULLINS

The peoples of the world not only will never love Big Brother, but they will soon dispose of him forever.

The program of the World Order remains the same; Divide and Conquer

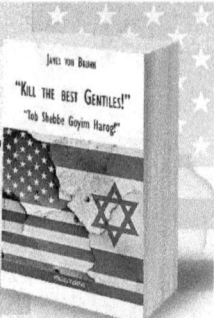

Omnia Veritas Ltd presents:

WE ARE WITNESSING today on the world stage a tragedy of enormous proportions: the calculated destruction of the White Race and the incomparable culture it represents

"KILL THE BEST GENTILES!"

"Tob Shebbe Goyim Harog!"

(THE TALMUD: Sanhedrin 59)

JAMES VON BRUNN

The most concentrated attacks on the White Race are occurring in the United States of America

Omnia Veritas Ltd presents:

The Real Victors of the Second World War

The World Conquerors

THE REAL WAR CRIMINALS

by

LOUIS MARSCHALKO

The Betrayal of America by the Secret Power.

www.ingramcontent.com/pod-product-compliance
Lightning Source LLC
Chambersburg PA
CBHW070249290326
41930CB00041B/2312